Brendon Moorhouse is an environmental and planning barrister practising at Six Pump Court, a Chambers recognised as one of the Countries' leading sets for environmental and planning law. He is regularly instructed in habitat and wildlife related matters and is frequently instructed in high profile permitting and planning related cases. He is a contributing author to Garner's Environmental Law.

A visiting research fellow and external member of the University of West of England's environmental law faculty, he is also a trustee and member of the global advisory panel of the Conservation Collective charity.

A Practical Guide to Habitats Law in Planning and Permitting in England

A Practical Guide to Habitats Law in Planning and Permitting in England

Brendon Moorhouse
Barrister, Six Pump Court, Temple

Law Brief Publishing

Published 2023 by Law Brief Publishing, an imprint of Law Brief Publishing Ltd
30 The Parks
Minehead
Somerset
TA24 8BT

www.lawbriefpublishing.com

Paperback: 978-1-914608-86-5

This book is dedicated to my late friend

Nicolas Gerasimidis

GLOSSARY OF TERMS

Berne Convention – The Convention on the Conservation of European Wildlife and Natural Habitats was adopted in Bern, Switzerland in 1979 and came into force in 1982.

Birds Directive – Council Directive 2009/147/EC (implemented originally as Directive 79/409/EEC before amendment and codification as 2009/147/EC.)

Emerald Network – A network of sites created under the Bern Convention designated for conservation purposes. SPAs and SACs are Emerald Network sites. Complaints in relation to breaches of the Convention can be made to the Standing Committee or its Bureau.

Environment Agency – A non-departmental public body established by The Environment Act 1995 and sponsored by DEFRA. It holds statutory responsibilities in relation to the protection and enhancement of the environment in England.

Environmental Impact Assessment Directive – Council Directive 2011/92/EU as amended by Directive 2014/52/EU

ESPOO (EIA) Convention – A UN Economic Commission for Europe convention setting out the obligations on parties to assess the environmental impact of certain activities and in relation to projects that are likely to have a significant adverse impact across national boundaries.

Joint Nature Conservancy Council (JNCC)- the body responsible for advising the UK Government on the designation and management of, amongst other things, SPAs, SACs, MPAs.

Habitats Directive – Council Directive 92/43/EEC

High Seas Treaty – Concluded on 4th March 2023, this treaty seeks to address conservation and sustainable use of marine biological diversity beyond national jurisdiction. (Also known as the Biodiversity Beyond National Jurisdiction treaty).

Marine Conservation Zones (MCZs) – a type of MPA designated to protect important areas

Marine Management Organisation (MMO) – An executive non-departmental public body created by the Marine and Coastal Access Act 2009 and tasked with management of England's marine and coastal environment.

Marine Protected Areas (MPAs) – these include marine SACs and SPAs, MCZs, SSSIs and Ramsar sites.

Nature Conservation Marine Protected Areas – A marine protected area that can be designated in Scottish territorial and offshore waters.

Natural England – Created by the provisions of the Natural Environment and Rural Communities Act 2006 Natural England has responsibility for England's natural environment.

Natural Resources Wales – The Welsh environmental and natural resources body, answerable to the Welsh Assembly Government.

Natura 2000 – An ecological network of protected areas including SPAs and SACs. This is now called the 'National Site Network' within the UK. (see also Emerald Network)

Natural Site Network – The name for areas formerly called Natura 2000 sites upon the UK leaving the EU in December 2020.

OSPAR Convention – The Convention for the Protection of the Marine Environment of the North-East Atlantic.

Ramsar Sites – Wetlands of international significance designated under the Ramsar Convention.[1] These are not 'natural site network' sites but carry the same protection as SACs and SPAs.

River Basin Management Plans (RBMPs) – These set legally binding locally specific environmental objectives underpinning water regulation that ought to be taken into account in planning and permitting decisions. Created pursuant to the Water Environment (Water Framework Directive) (England and Wales) Regulations 2017.

SEA Directive – The Strategic Environmental Assessment Directive 2001/42/EC.

Sites of Special Scientific Interest (SSSIs) – Sites designated under the Wildlife and Countryside Act 1981.

Special Areas of Conservation (SACs) – Areas designated under the Habitats Directive as making a significant contribution to conserving habitats and species.

Special Protection Areas (SPAs) - Areas designated for the protection of birds designated under the Birds Directive. They are part of the Natura 2000 network since 1994.

UN Convention on the Law of the Sea (UNCLOS) – Originally this treaty was formulated in 1958 and (with amendments and additions) covers issues such as freedom of navigation, exclusive economic zones as well as fishing and conservation of living resources.

---

1 The Ramsar Convention was adopted in the Iranian city of Ramsar in 1971 and implemented in 1975.

CONTENTS

Introduction		1
Chapter One	An Overview of Habitats Protection	5
Chapter Two	Planning – Environmental Impact Assessment	21
Chapter Three	Marine Works – Environmental Impact Assessment	45
Chapter Four	General Biodiversity Duty	71
Chapter Five	The Habitats Directive and Regulations	75
	Part 1: Habitats Regulations – The designation and management of the National Site Network	75
	Part 2: Plans or Projects affecting the National Site Network	85
Chapter Six	Habitat and Biodiversity Trends	107

INTRODUCTION

The system of habitat and wildlife protection in England can properly be described as complicated. In part this is because the existing protections of flora, fauna and their habitats have taken place through a patchwork process of layering different regimes over one another – some offering greater degrees of protection than others and each broadly operating in distinct ways. It is an area of law that has evolved alongside evolving scientific understanding, and where changes are often seen to have political consequences that themselves drive further change. The law, like the habitats and wildlife it seeks to protect, is constantly changing.

The consequence of the complicated layers of habitats and wildlife law is that it can be difficult to understand how the main provisions apply and interrelate. As an practical overview, this book aims to fill that gap, at the same time as providing the reader with a sound footing in this area of law and an understanding of how it has evolved.

The aim of this book is to cover the core provisions for the protection of endangered plants and animals, the habitats that sustain them and the habitats that are distinctive in their own right, as provided by the Habitats Directive[1] and other ancillary regimes such as the Environmental Impact Assessment process.

The Habitats directive, together with the Birds Directive[2], has become a central part of the decision-making process affecting many planning applications, infrastructure projects, environmental permits issued under the Environmental Permitting Regulations and many licences issued, for example those issued by the Marine Management Organisation.

---

1 Council Directive 92/43/EEC of 21st May 1992.

2 Council Directive 79/409/EEC that was amended in 2009 becoming Directive 2009/147/EC.

The book is centred on English Law, although many of the principles will have application and possibly persuasive authority in other UK jurisdictions. The devolution of a national Government into the Scottish Parliament, National Assembly for Wales in 1998 and Northern Irish devolution following the Good Friday Agreement included the devolution of environmental legislative powers to each jurisdiction. While there remains a significant overlap between English and Welsh laws, for example, The Conservation of Habitats and Species Regulations 2017 (SI 2017 No 1012), there remain significant departures. The Environment (Wales) Act 2016 and the Well-being of Future Generations Act 2015 are unique Welsh primary legislation that affect both the administration and legal decision-making processes for decisions made in Wales.[3] A significant body of statutory instruments have been made that are unique to Wales, which will not be discussed in depth in this book.

Even though the UK has left the EU, the Habitats Directive remains largely in force in a similar way to its operation within EU countries and the Regulations made pursuant to the Habitats Directive remain fully in force.

The book is written with chapter headings designed to be practically useful to guide a reader through key aspects of the practical application of habitats law.

As a Practical Guide to Habitats Law, this book does not pretend to be exhaustive. While every effort has been made to ensure that this book is

---

3 For example the Welsh First Minister's decision to reject the M4 Corridor Around Newport, citing consideration of both unique aspects of Welsh legislation at paras 6.20 and 6.23 of the decision letter (4th June 2019).

up to date as of the summer of 2023, it is a rapidly evolving highly regulated area.[4]

The law stated in this book is believed to be up-to-date on 15th November 2023.

4 A good example of the rapid pace of evolution of the law, at the time of completing the book, the Government is proposing to change the basis of regulating nutrient neutrality in their Levelling-up and Regeneration Bill.

CHAPTER ONE

AN OVERVIEW OF HABITATS PROTECTION

A 'habitat' can be defined as the natural home or environment of an animal, plant or other organism. It follows from that definition, that almost any planning or permitting decision is capable of having some effect on the home and environment of organisms that rely on them directly or indirectly.

By way of overview, the treaties and laws relating to 'habitat protection' in fact are often aimed at the protection of specific species while others are directed towards protecting specific habitat types. Some regulation is aimed at protecting the environment from polluting material.

A key part of wildlife and habitat protection is the Habitats Directive that, as implemented in the UK, draws on a number of threads of environmental protection legislation and treaties that have developed over the years in what could be perceived as an ad hoc manner. Many of these threads remain 'in force' and are administered and regulated by different bodies. The intention of the following paragraphs is to provide a concise context to the current legal framework and the current system of 'habitat protection' that is now underpinned by species and 'National Site Network' protections as well as the environmental assessment provisions commonly encountered in planning applications.

The following sections of this overview chapter of the guide will summarise important treaties and legislation. These including the Berne Convention on the Conservation of European Wildlife and Natural Habitats, the 'Birds Directive', the 'Habitats Directive,' the Ramsar Convention on Wetlands of International Importance, Marine Habitat Provisions as well as Environmental Impact Assessment provisions.

Together, these form the main regulation applicable to habitat protection.

The Berne Convention

Many Habitats Directive principles, and therefore the concepts that underpin the Conservation of Habitats and Species Regulations 2017 (SI 2017/1012) ('the Habitats Regulations'), derive from the Berne Convention on the Conservation of European Wildlife and Natural Habitats (1979). The Berne Convention aims to protect the natural heritage of Europe and some African countries[5]. It was ratified by both members of the Council of Europe and also non-members.

The treaty not only prescribed certain acts against protected species, but also required Contracting Parties to implement the necessary legislative measures to ensure the conservation of the habitats of the protected flora and fauna.

From a UK perspective, the treaty was signed in September 1979, ratified in May 1982 and came into force the following September. It was implemented through the adoption of Natural Nature Reserves[6] and Sites of Special Scientific Interest[7]. Both of these types of designated areas are overseen by Natural England.

Article 1 of the Berne Convention sets out three objectives:

- to conserve wild flora and fauna and their natural habitats

[5] African signatories include Burkina Faso, Morocco, Tunisia, and Senegal

[6] Prior to this the National Parks and Access to the Countryside Act 1949 made provision for National Parks, managed by a National Parks Commission, a role now occupied by Natural England in England and Natural Resources Wales in Wales.

[7] Introduced by Section 28 of the Wildlife and Countryside Act 1981.

- to promote cooperation between states
- to give particular attention to endangered and vulnerable species including endangered and vulnerable migratory species

The Chapters, Articles and Appendixes of the Berne Convention that followed made provision that Contracting Parties should take measures for the protection of designated habitats[8] and designated species[9]. Appendix I lists 'strictly protected flora' and Appendix II lists 'strictly protected fauna'. Appendix III lists 'protected fauna species' that hold a lesser degree of protection. Habitat protection under the Berne Convention was further strengthened by, amongst others, Resolution No 1 (1989) of the Standing Committee of the Berne Convention that placed obligations on signatory states to take 'necessary measures' to protect habitats and by Resolution No 5 (1998) that set up a 'Network of Areas of Special Conservation Interest (Emerald Network).'

Within the EU structure, the 'Emerald Network' of sites was replicated by the 'Natura 2000' Birds and Habitat Directive sites (explained further below) and the necessary protection afforded by those Directives.

On leaving the EU, the UK through the agency of the Joint Nature Conservation Committee (JNCC) ensured all Natura 2000 sites' information was registered as part of the Emerald Network in order to meet the UK's continuing obligations under the Berne Convention.

At a higher level, the Standing Committee of the Bern Convention or its Bureau are able to receive and consider complaints about failure by a nation state to properly implement the protections of the Convention.[10]

---

8 Chapter 2 – particular attention was to be given to habitats containing protected species or important for migratory birds.

9 Chapter 3 and Appendixes.

10 For example, T-PVS/Files (2014) 38, a series of complaints brought against France, Ireland and the UK in relation to alleged failure to protect

The Birds Directive

The Birds Directive was the first environmental legislation implemented by the then European Economic Community in April 1979. Upon formation of the European Union and amendment it became Council Directive 79/409/EEC.

The cornerstone of the Birds Directive was the creation of Special Protection Areas (SPAs). Designated SPAs are aimed at protecting wild birds from urban sprawl, intrusive transport networks, intensive agriculture, and other environmental harm, for example, the use of pesticides that diminish food supplies.

The Birds Directive makes provision for the protection of all species of naturally occurring birds in the wild state within the European territory and protects birds, their eggs and habitats.[11] The legal obligation is on Member States to *'take the requisite measures to preserve, maintain or re-establish a sufficient diversity and area of habitats.'* That legal obligation extends to the requirement to create *'protected areas,'* the upkeep and management in accordance with the ecological needs of habitats inside and outside the protected zones, and the creation of and re-establishment of destroyed biotopes. A biotope is synonymous with a habitat, being the assemblage of plants and animals necessary to maintain the organism, in this case the bird(s), subject to protection.[12]

Of approximately 500 species of Birds naturally occurring within Europe, 194 species were identified as being particularly threatened and were listed within Annex 1 of the Birds Directive. Member States, pursuant to Article 4 of the Birds Directive, are required to monitor

---

the Eurasian Badger. In the UK's case the complaint, in relation to the 'badger cull', was rejected. More recently Azerbaijan has brought a complaint against Armenia for biodiversity and environmental destruction consequent on the war between both states.

11 Article 1.

12 Article 3

trends and variations to population levels for background evaluations, and to classify special protection areas in the most suitable territories for the conservation of these Annex 1-listed species.

Article 4 requires Member States to take similar protective measures for regularly occurring migratory species not listed in Annex 1, and to pay particular attention to the protection of wetlands and wetlands of international importance.[13] Article 4 also sets a legal requirement on Member States to avoid the pollution or deterioration of habitats.

By way of overview, the Birds Directive also makes provision for Member States to implement protection for 82 Annex 2 species of birds that can be hunted. Annex 2 limits the periods when hunting is permissible and restricts activities that directly threaten birds in general, save for 26 species listed in Annex 3. Annex 4 sets out provisions for sustainable management of birds including outlawing non-selective and largescale killing of birds especially by methods shown in Annex 4.[14]

Protections afforded to Annex 1 birds under the Birds Directive are largely, although not completely, synonymous to those for other species listed under the Habitats Directive.

The Habitats Directive

The Habitats Directive was the then European Economic Communities' (EEC) response to the Berne Convention. Council Directive 92/43/EEC on the 'Conservation of natural habitats and of wild fauna and flora' was adopted by the European Community in 1992. The Habitats Directive was retained upon the formation of the European Union in 1993. These

---

[13] There is an overlap with the Ramsar Convention obligations afforded by these requirements.

[14] These provisions were implemented in Great Britain by the Wildlife and Countryside Act 1981. Of historical interest, the structure and approach adopted in the Protection of Birds Act 1954 was largely followed and replicated by the EEC in the Birds Directive.

provisions largely remain in force as 'retained law' following the UK's departure from the EU.

The purpose of the Habitats Directive is the conservation of a wide range of animal and plant species, and the protection of characteristic habitat types that are protected in their own right. There are six Annex's within the Directive. Of those, Annex I and Annex II are regularly referred to in relation to habitat and wildlife protection.

Annex I of the Habitats Directive lists 233 European natural habitat types, including 71 'priority habitats' – those habitat types in danger of disappearance and whose natural range mainly fell within the territory of European Union countries. These habitat ranges include coastal habitats, for example, Atlantic and Continental salt marsh and salt meadows; coastal and inland dunes; freshwater habitats; temperate heath and scrub; certain grassland formations; bogs and fens; rocky habitats and forests.[15]

Annex II of the Habitats Directive lists approximately 900 animal and plant species of community interest whose conservation requires designation of Special Areas of Conservation (SAC). The types of species include invertebrates, for example freshwater pearl mussels; fish, for example the Atlantic salmon; amphibians such as the great crested newt; mammals, examples of which include certain bat species, otters, harbour porpoise and grey seals; and lower and higher plant species including petalwort and floating water-plantain.

Within England and Wales, the principal legislation implementing the Habitats Directive is the Conservation of Habitats and Species Regulations 2017 (SI 2017/1012). ('the Habitats Regulations').

---

[15] The EU prepared various Interpretation Manuals, for example, 'Interpretation Manual of European Union Habitats – EUR28' published in April 2013, to assist in identifying suitable habitats and specific areas to protect.

Ramsar Convention

The Convention on Wetlands of International Importance especially as Waterfowl Habitat (the 'Ramsar Convention') was created in 1971 in the Iranian city bearing the Convention name.

The objectives of the Ramsar Convention were stipulated and described as being constituted of 'three pillars.' These are to work towards the wise use of all Contracting Party wetlands, to designate suitable wetlands for the list of Wetlands of International Importance (the 'Ramsar List') and to ensure their effective management and to co-operate internationally on transboundary wetlands.

The UK ratified the Ramsar Convention and designated its first site in 1976. The designation of Ramsar Sites is formalised within England through their designation as having SSSI status and therefore protection under the Wildlife and Countryside Act 1981.

Of greater significance for wider habitat protection in relation to Ramsar Sites is the Ministerial Statement of Mr Michael Meacher on 13th November 2000[16]:

> *24. Local planning authorities are expected to extend the scope of their appropriate assessments when carrying out Regulation 50 reviews on Natura 2000*[17] *sites to consider the effects on coincident or overlapping Ramsar sites. Where the planning authority reaches the conclusion that there would be no adverse effect on the integrity of the Natura 2000 site from allowing the consent to proceed, but there would be an adverse effect on integrity on the Ramsar site, it should consider whether to issue a modification or revocation order using powers available under Section 97 of the Town and Country Planning Act 1990. In cases*

16 Hansard 13th November 2000: Columns: 491W and 492W.

17 An ecological network of protected areas including SPAs and SACs designated under the Birds and Habitats Directives. This is now called the 'National Site Network' within the UK.

where the authority considers modification or revocation is warranted, the Government will consider reimbursing local authorities where the costs were high, where the action taken was no more than necessary to remove the risk to the site, and less costly alternatives have been fully explored.

25. Local planning authorities are expected to adopt a similar approach where listed Ramsar sites are not within the Natura 2000 network, by carrying out an appropriate assessment analogous to that required by Regulation 50 and by issuing modification or revocation orders under Section 97 of the Town and Country Planning Act 1990, at the earliest opportunity following the listing of a Ramsar site. Where the integrity of a Ramsar site would be adversely affected by the full implementation of an extant consent and modification or revocation of the consent is warranted, the Government will again consider reimbursing local authorities where the costs were high, where the action taken was no more than necessary to remove the risk to the site, and less costly alternatives have been fully explored.

26. The Government expect competent authorities, other than planning authorities, to use whatever review powers are available within the regimes they administer to address any potential adverse effects on the integrity of listed Ramsar sites from extant consents by adopting a general approach analogous to that advocated for planning authorities in paragraphs 24 & 25 above.

Ramsar sites are, in practice, protected to the same extent as sites designated under the Habitats and Birds Directive This is both in a planning context as well as in other decisions such as permitting decisions that are likely to have a significant effect on the site.

The JNCC maintains information for all UK Ramsar sites.

Marine Protection Areas

The term Marine Protected Areas includes marine areas designated for protection under a variety of different mechanisms. These include SACs, SPAs and SSSIs with a marine component, Ramsar sites and also Marine Conservation Zones (MCZs).

Marine protected areas include areas within UK territorial waters (up to 12 nautical miles,) and offshore areas within the exclusive economic zone (up to 200 nautical miles.)

Marine Conservation Zones are created by DEFRA pursuant to Section 116 of the Marine and Coastal Access Act 2009, listing the features that are to be protected and also setting the conservation objective(s) of the MCZ. The designations are made for the purpose of conserving marine flora or fauna, marine habitats, or for types of habitats and/or features of geological or geomorphological interest.[18]

There is a general duty placed upon public authorities that have any function, the exercise of which is capable of affecting other than insignificantly, the protected features of an MCZ or any ecological or geomorphological process on which the conservation of any protected feature of an MCZ is wholly or in part dependent. The obligation placed upon public authorities is to exercise their functions so as to best further the conservation objectives, or where it is not possible to further those objectives, to exercise their functions in a manner that least hinders the achievement of those objectives.[19] There are duties of notification to the Marine Management Organisation (MMO)[20] by a public authority where a relevant event takes place. A relevant event includes any act in relation to the public authority exercising its functions, which the

---

[18] Section 117 Marine and Coastal Access Act 2009.

[19] Section 125 Marine and Coastal Access Act 2009.

[20] In Wales and Scotland the notification requirements are to the respective Ministers.

authority believes to be an offence and which the authority considers will or may significantly hinder the achievement of the conservation objectives of the MCZ.

The Marine and Coastal Act 2009 also introduced the concept of 'Marine Plans' that are created by the MMO with a view to setting priorities and the direction of future development, informing sustainable use of marine resources, and assisting in determining where any new development is most appropriate within the plan area.

A central domestic regulation in relation to offshore marine habitats protection is the Conservation of Offshore Marine Habitats and Species Regulations 2017 (SI 2017/1013) ('Offshore Marine Habitats Regulations') that applies to areas beyond the 12 nautical mile limit. The Habitats Regulations (SI 2017/2012) are applicable to the inshore area up to 12 nautical miles.

Sites of Special Scientific Interest

In England, Natural England have responsibility for the designation and management of Sites of Special Scientific Interest ('SSSIs').[21] Sites are designated because they contain features of special interest, by reason of their flora, fauna, geology, and physiographical features.[22] There are over 4,000 such sites in England. A feature of SSSIs is that they only cover land above the mean low water mark, or estuarial waters, and so SSSIs have limited interaction with many marine works.

Once a site has been notified by Natural England it attracts protection of the features, even while the formal confirmation process is concluded.

Once notified, Natural England have a duty to achieve 'favourable condition' status for SSSIs, meaning that the habitats and features of the

---

21 In Wales, Natural Resources Wales, have responsibility. In Scotland it is Scottish Natural Heritage.

22 Section 28 Wildlife and Countryside Act 1981.

site are in a healthy state and are being conserved by appropriate management. The notification process sets out operations which the owner or occupier of a site is required to seek written permission from Natural England before they can carry out. Such permission may be granted with conditions and be for a time-limited period.[23] Operations may also be carried out in accordance with the terms of an agreement made under Section 7 of the Natural Environment and Rural Communities Act 2006 with a person having an interest in the land, or in accordance with a management scheme for the site.

In planning terms, the effect of the designation of an area as a SSSI provides restrictions on permitted development. It is also a material consideration within the planning process. The Current version of the National Planning Policy Framework provides[24]:

> *Development on land within or outside a Site of Special Scientific Interest, and which is likely to have an adverse effect on it (either individually or in combination with other developments), should not normally be permitted. The only exception is where the benefits of the development in the location proposed clearly outweigh both its likely impact on the features of the site that make it of special scientific interest, and any broader impacts on the national network of Sites of Special Scientific Interest;*

Criminal liability can attach to certain breaches of the requirements to protect SSSIs.

Retained Law – European Union Withdrawal

The European Union has had a central role in defining UK and English Habitats protection regulation. On the 31st December 2020 at 11pm, the United Kingdom left the European Union. Since then, the European

---

23 Section 28E Wildlife and Countryside Act 1981.

24 Para 180(b) NPPF 2021.

Union (Withdrawal) Act 2018 governs the role which legislation and case-law derived from EU legal instruments continues to have in the UK.

Section 2 of the European Union (Withdrawal) Act 2018 retains EU-derived domestic legislation 'as it has effect in domestic law immediately before IP completion day, continues to have effect in domestic law on and after IP completion day.'[25] Sections 3 and 4 respectively dealt with savings of directly applicable EU law and the saving of rights, powers, liabilities, obligations, restrictions, remedies and procedures.

The applicability of the Habitats Regulations was specifically considered in the case of *Harris and Harris v Environment Agency and Natural England* [2022] EWHC 2264 (Admin) with Johnson J, in summary, finding that: (i) the Habitats Regulations, passed under Section 2(2) of the European Communities Act 1972 is EU-derived domestic legislation and continues to have effect in domestic law pursuant to Section 2(1) of the European Union (Withdrawal) Act 2018, (ii) that the Habitats Directive is not 'direct EU legislation' and does not form part of domestic law, (iii) obligations that were recognised and available in domestic law continue and are recognised and available in domestic law (iv) the precautionary principle is a retained general principle if EU law pursuant to Section 6(7) of the European Union (Withdrawal) Act 2018.

In relation to the status of previously decided European Court (CJEU) decisions, the Court of Appeal has confirmed that such decisions are still binding. While the Supreme Court and Court of Appeal[26] has the power to depart from CJEU case law, it can only do so on the same basis that

[25] 'IP Completion day' means 31st December 2021 at 11.00 p.m. (Section 39 of the European Union (Withdrawal Agreement) Act 2020.)

[26] Section 6(4) European Union (Withdrawal) Act 2018.

the Supreme Court can depart from its own precedent. Such power must be 'exercised with great caution.'[27]

Environmental Impact Assessment

Separate to the Habitats Directive, the EEC created an Environmental Impact Assessment Directive[28] that came into force in 1985. It has been updated four times and the main law is now within Directive 2011/92/EU as amended by Directive 2014/52/EU.

In England these were implemented by the Town and Country Planning (Environmental Impact Assessment) Regulations 2017 (SI 2017/571) (the 'EIA Regulations'), which remain in force post Brexit and apply to certain planning applications and regulated marine activities. There are corresponding Welsh regulations.[29]

An Environmental Impact Assessment (EIA) is required to be submitted for certain specified types of development listed in Schedule 1 of the EIA Regulations.

Schedule 2 of the EIA Regulations identifies categories of development in what are described as 'sensitive areas,' for example SSSIs, national parks or Habitats Regulation Sites, or where the development exceeds the criteria listed in the schedule. Should a potential development fall within such a site or fulfil the criteria, the planning authority or Secretary of State is required to screen the application using selection criteria set out in Schedule 3 of the EIA Regulations to determine whether the development is likely to have a significant effect on the environment. In screening such an application particular regard has to be paid to factors that include the use of natural resources, in particular land, soil, water

27 Kanaka Durga Chelluri v Air India Ltd [2021] EWCA Civ 1953, following Tunein inc v Warner Music and Sony Music Entertainment [2021] EWCA Civ 441.

28 Environmental Impact Assessment Directive (85/337/EEC)

29 SI 2017/567.

and biodiversity,' 'pollution and nuisances' and 'the risk to human health (for example, due to water contamination or air pollution).'[30]

There are separate Environmental Impact Assessment regulatory provisions relevant to planning applications made for, amongst others, harbours, highways and transport[31] (that amends primary legislation, such as the Harbours Act 1964, the Highways Act 1980) and certain agricultural applications.[32] For marine works the Marine Works (Environmental Impact Assessment) Regulations 2007[33] are applicable and The Infrastructure Planning (Environmental Impact Assessment) Regulations 2017[34] are applicable to nationally significant infrastructure projects.

Strategic Environmental Assessment

The Environmental Assessment of Plans and Programmes Regulations 2004[35] (as amended) was implemented in the UK to give effect to EU Directive 2001/42/EC, known as the 'SEA Directive,' and applies to plans and programmes adopted by an authority at a national, regional or local level or that are prepared by an authority for adoption through legislative procedure by Parliament or Government.

In summary, the assessments are intended to provide a high-level environmental consideration to plans or programmes that can include both planning development, for example local or marine plans, but are

---

30 Town and Country Planning (Environmental Impact Assessment) Regulations 2017 (SI 2017/571) Schedule 3(1).

31 Environmental Impact Assessment (Miscellaneous Amendments Relating to Harbours, Highways and Transport) Regulations 2017 (SI 2017/2010)

32 Environmental Impact Assessment (Agriculture)(England)(No2) Regulations 2006 (SI 2006/2522) as amended.

33 SI 2007/1518

34 SI 2017/572

35 SI 2004/1633

also applicable to many other sectors including agriculture, forestry, fisheries, energy, industry, transport, waste management, telecommunications and tourism where the plan or programme is likely to have significant environmental effects.

Summary / Concluding the Introduction

The various provisions set out above are an overview of the main safeguard provisions in relation to the protection of habitats in England, and also in many cases a history of how they arose. The following chapters include a detailed examination of the central features of said provisions.

CHAPTER TWO

PLANNING – ENVIRONMENTAL IMPACT ASSESSMENT

The Environmental Impact Assessment process (EIA) is a key aspect of regulation within the planning regime aimed at taking environmental factors into account in certain developments. Planning development, as defined by Section 55 of the Town and Country Planning Act 1990, is capable of having a considerable impact on habitats and biodiversity. Therefore the EIA process provides an important part of the safeguarding system designed to ensure that such factors are fully taken into account when development decisions are taken. It also permits public participation in the process. The legislative starting point for considering these issues in England, starts with the Town and Country Planning (Environmental Impact Assessment) Regulations 2017.[36] (the 'EIA Regulations'). Additionally, there is Planning Practice Guidance on Environmental Impact Assessment[37] that should be consulted.

Is an Environmental Impact Assessment Necessary?

An early and fundamental step in the planning process is to determine whether the proposed development amounts to an EIA development within the meaning of the EIA Regulations. This is fundamental since, pursuant to Regulation 3 of the EIA Regulations the relevant planning authority, the Secretary of State or an Inspector must not grant planning permission or subsequent consent for an EIA development unless an EIA has been carried out in respect of that development.

---

[36] SI 2017/571.

[37] Published 13th May 2020.

The EIA Regulations contain two schedules relevant to deciding whether an EIA assessment is necessary.

Schedule 1

A development that falls within the description provided under Schedule 1 of the EIA Regulations always requires an EIA.[38] There are twenty-four types of development within Schedule 1 and any development that is carried proposed that is listed in Schedule 1 requires a mandatory EIA Assessment:

1 Crude oil refineries (excluding undertakings manufacturing only lubricants from crude oil) and installations for the gasification and liquefaction of 500 tonnes or more of coal or bituminous shale per day.

2(1) Thermal power stations and other combustion installations with a heat

output of 300 megawatts or more.

(2) Nuclear power stations and other nuclear reactors (except research

installations for the production and conversion of fissionable and fertile materials, whose maximum power does not exceed 1 kilowatt continuous thermal load).

3(1) Installations for the reprocessing of irradiated nuclear fuel.

(2) Installations designed—

(a) for the production or enrichment of nuclear fuel;

[38] Save for an exemption provided by the Secretary of State made under Regulation 63 of the EIA Regulations.

(b) for the processing of irradiated nuclear fuel or high level radioactive waste;

(c) for the final disposal of irradiated nuclear fuel;

(d) solely for the final disposal of radioactive waste;

(e) solely for the storage (planned for more than ten years) of irradiated nuclear fuels or radioactive waste in a different site than the production site.

4(1) Integrated works for the initial smelting of cast iron and steel.

(2) Installations for the production of non-ferrous crude metals from ore, concentrates or secondary raw materials by metallurgical, chemical or electrolytic processes.

5 Installations for the extraction of asbestos and for the processing and transformation of asbestos and products containing asbestos—

(a) for asbestos cement products, with an annual production of more than 20,000 tonnes of finished products;

(b) for friction material, with an annual production of more than 50 tonnes of finished products; and

(c) for other uses of asbestos, utilisation of more than 200 tonnes per year.

6 Integrated chemical installations, that is to say, installations for the manufacture on an industrial scale of substances using chemical conversion processes, in which several units are juxtaposed and are functionally linked to one another and which are—

(a) for the production of basic organic chemicals;

(b) for the production of basic inorganic chemicals;

(c) for the production of phosphorous-, nitrogen- or potassium based fertilisers (simple or compound fertilisers);

(d) for the production of basic plant health products and of biocides;

(e) for the production of basic pharmaceutical products using a chemical or biological process; or

(f) for the production of explosives.

7(1) Construction of lines for long distance railway traffic and of airports with a basic runway length of 2,100 metres or more.

(2) Construction of motorways and express roads.

(3) Construction of a new road of four or more lanes, or realignment and/or widening of an existing road of two lanes or less so as to provide four or more lanes, where such new road, or realigned and/or widened section of road, would be 10 kilometres or more in a continuous length.

8(1) Inland waterways and ports for inland waterway traffic which permit the passage of vessels of over 1,350 tonnes.

(2) Trading ports, piers for loading and unloading connected to land and outside ports (excluding ferry piers) which can take vessels of over 1,350 tonnes.

9 Waste disposal installations for the incineration, chemical treatment (as defined in Annex I to Directive 2008/98/EC of the European Parliament and of the Council on waste, as last amended by Directive (EU) 2018/851 under heading D9), or landfill of hazardous waste as defined in Article 3(2) of that Directive.

10 Waste disposal installations for the incineration or chemical treatment (as defined in Annex I to Directive 2008/98/EC under heading D9) of non-hazardous waste with a capacity exceeding 100 tonnes per day.

11 Groundwater abstraction or artificial groundwater recharge schemes where the annual volume of water abstracted or recharged is equivalent to or exceeds 10 million cubic metres.

12(1) Works for the transfer of water resources, other than piped drinking water, between river basins where the transfer aims at preventing possible shortages of water and where the amount of water transferred exceeds 100 million cubic metres per year.

(2) In all other cases, works for the transfer of water resources, other than piped drinking water, between river basins where the multi annual average flow of the basin of abstraction exceeds 2,000 million cubic metres per year and where the amount of water transferred exceeds 5% of this flow.

13 Waste-water treatment plants with a capacity exceeding 150,000 population equivalent as defined in Article 2(6) of Council Directive 91/271/EEC of 21 May 1991 concerning urban waste-water treatment.

14 Extraction of petroleum and natural gas for commercial purposes where the amount extracted exceeds 500 tonnes per day in the case of petroleum and 500,000 cubic metres per day in the case of gas.

15 Dams and other installations designed for the holding back or permanent storage of water, where a new or additional amount of water held back or stored exceeds 10 million cubic metres.

16 Pipelines with a diameter of more than 800 millimetres and a length of more than 40 kilometres for the transport of—

(a) gas, oil or chemicals; or

(b) carbon dioxide streams for the purposes of geological storage, including associated booster stations.

17 Installations for the intensive rearing of poultry or pigs with more than—

(a) 85,000 places for broilers or 60,000 places for hens;

(b) 3,000 places for production pigs (over 30 kg); or

(c) 900 places for sows.

18 Industrial plants for—

(a) the production of pulp from timber or similar fibrous materials; or

(b) the production of paper and board with a production capacity exceeding 200 tonnes per day.

19 Quarries and open cast mining where the surface of the site exceeds 25 hectares, or peat extraction where the surface of the site exceeds 150 hectares.

20 Construction of overhead electrical power lines with a voltage of 220 kV or more and a length of more than 15 km.

21 Installations for storage of petroleum, petrochemical or chemical products with a capacity of 200,000 tonnes or more.

22 Storage sites pursuant to Directive 2009/31/EC of the European Parliament and of the Council of 23 April 2009 on the geological storage of carbon dioxide.

23 Installations for the capture of carbon dioxide streams for the purposes of geological storage pursuant to Directive 2009/31/EC from installations referred to in this Schedule, or where the total yearly capture of carbon dioxide is 1.5 mega tonnes or more

24 Any change to or extension of development listed in this Schedule where such a change or extension in itself meets the thresholds, if any, or description of development set out in this Schedule.

It is self-evident that the above list generally relates to significant projects where the need for an EIA is more likely to be clear-cut. More likely to be contentious, in a legal sense, are Schedule 2 developments. Ultimately, whether a particular development falls within one of the schedule descriptions, has been determined to be a question of fact for the planning authority to determine, subject to the usual *Wednesbury*[39] challenge.[40]

Schedule 2

Schedule 2 development is defined as development, other than an exempt development, of a description mentioned in column 1 of the table in Schedule 2 of the EIA Regulations, where either any part of that development is to be carried out in a 'sensitive area', or any applicable threshold or criterion in the corresponding part of column 2 of that table respectively exceeded or met in relation to that development.[41]

A 'sensitive area' is defined in the EIA Regulations as land notified as a SSSI under Section 28 of the Wildlife and Countryside Act 1981, a National Park within the meaning of the Natural Parks and Access to

[39] Associated Provincial Picture Houses Ltd v Wednesbury Corporation (1948) 1 KB 223.

[40] See for example R v Swale Borough Council ex parte the RSPB [1991] JPL 39

[41] Regulation 2 EIA Regulations SI 2017/571.

Countryside Act 1949, the Broads, a property appearing in the UNESCO World Heritage List under article 11(2), a scheduled monument within the meaning of the Ancient Monuments and Archaeological Areas Act 1979, an area of outstanding natural beauty as designated by an order under Section 82 of the Countryside and Rights of Way Act 2000 or a European Site.[42]

The developments listed include:

1 Agriculture and aquaculture

Use of uncultivated or semi-natural areas for intensive agricultural purposes, where the site exceeds 0.5 hectare. Water management projects for agriculture, including irrigation and land drainage projects where the site exceeds 1 hectare. Intensive livestock installations, unless included in Schedule 1, where the area of new floorspace exceeds 500 square metres. Intensive fish farming if the development is designed to produce more than ten tonnes of dead weight fish per year. Any reclamation of land from the sea.

2 Extractive industry

Quarries, open cast mining and peat extraction, unless included in Schedule 1, and underground mining, unless the development is of ancillary structures where the new floorspace does not exceed 1,000 square metres. All extraction of minerals by fluvial or marine dredging. Deep drilling, in particular geothermal drilling, drilling to store nuclear waste and drilling for water supplies unless the drilling is for soil stability purposes where the drilling works exceed 1 hectare or where geothermal or nuclear waste drilling is within 100 metres of controlled waters. Surface

[42] The wording is taken from the Regulations where the definition of a European Site has been changed in the interpretation regulation to take changes brought about through Brexit into account.

industrial installations for the extraction of coal, petroleum, natural gas and ores, as well as bituminous shale where the development exceeds 05 hectares.

3 Energy industry

Industrial installations for the production of electricity, steam and hot water, unless included in Schedule 1, that exceed 0.5 hectares. Industrial installations for carrying gas, steam and hot water that exceed 1 hectare. Surface storage of natural gas, the underground storage of combustible gases and the surface storage of fossil fuels where the area of any new building, deposit or structure exceeds 500 square metres or any new building, deposit or structure is to be within 100 metres of controlled waters. Industrial briquetting of coal and lignite where new floorspace exceeds 1,000 square metres. Installations for the processing and storage of radioactive waste, unless included in Schedule 1, where new floorspace exceeds 1,000 square metres or where a permit would be required under certain provisions of the Environmental Permitting (England and Wales) Regulations 2016. Installations for hydroelectric energy production where the installation is designed to produce more than 0.5 megawatts. Wind farms where the installation has more than two turbines of the hub height of any turbine or other structure exceeds 15 metres. Installations for the capture of carbon dioxide streams for the purposes of geological storage pursuant to Directive 2009/31/EC from installations not included in Schedule 1.

4 Production and processing of metals

Where the new floorspace exceeds 1,000 square metres, the following are covered by schedule 2. Installations for the production of pig iron or steel (primary or secondary fusion) including continuous casting. Installations for the processing of ferrous metals including hot-rolling mills, smitheries with hammers and application of protective fused metal coats. Ferrous metal foundries. Installations for the smelting, including the alloyage, of non-ferrous metals, excluding precious metals, including recovered products (refining, foundry casting, etc). Installations for surface treatment of metals and plastic materials using an electrolytic or chemical process. Manufacture and assembly of motor vehicles and manufacture of motor-vehicle engines. Shipyards. Installations for the construction and repair of aircraft. Manufacture of railway equipment. Swaging by explosives. Installations for the roasting and sintering of metallic ores.

5 Mineral Industry

Where the new floorspace exceeds 1,000 square metres, the following are covered by schedule 2: Coke ovens (dry coal distillation). Installations for the manufacture of cement. Installations for the production of asbestos and the manufacture of asbestos-based products, unless included in Schedule 1. Installations for the manufacture of glass including glass fibre. Installations for smelting mineral substances including the production of mineral fibres. Manufacture of ceramic products by burning, in particular roofing tiles, bricks, refractory bricks, tiles, stoneware or porcelain.

6 Chemical industry unless included in Schedule 1

Where the new floorspace exceeds 1,000 square metres treatment of intermediate products and production of chemicals and Production of pesticides and pharmaceutical products, paint and varnishes, elastomers and peroxides.

The storage facilities for petroleum, petrochemical and chemical products where the area of any new building exceeds 0.05 hectares or more than 200 tonnes of petroleum, petrochemical or chemical products are to be stored at any one time.

7 Food industry

Where the new floorspace exceeds 1,000 square metres, the following are covered by schedule 2: The manufacture of vegetable and animal oils and fats, packing and canning of animal and vegetable products, the manufacture of dairy products, brewing and malting, confectionery and syrup manufacture, installations for the slaughter of animals, industrial starch manufacturing installations, fish-meal and fish-oil factories and sugar factories.

8 Textiles, leather wood and paper industries

Where the new floorspace exceeds 1,000 square metres, the following are covered by schedule 2: Industrial plants for the production of paper and board, unless included in Schedule 1, plants for the pre-treatment (operations such as washing, bleaching, mercerisation) or dyeing of fibres or textiles, plants for the tanning of hides and skins and cellulose-processing and production installations.

9 Rubber industry

The manufacture and treatment of elastomer-based products where the area of new floorspace exceeds 1,000 square metres.

10 Infrastructure projects

Industrial estate development projects that exceed 5 hectares. Urban development projects, including the construction of shopping centres and car parks, sports stadiums, leisure centres and multiplex cinemas where the development includes more than 1 hectare of urban development which is not dwellinghouse development, the development includes more than 150 dwellings, or the overall development exceeds 5 hectares. Construction of intermodal trans-shipment facilities and of intermodal terminals unless included in Schedule 1 and where the development exceeds 0.5 hectares. Construction of railways, unless included in Schedule 1 and where the works exceed 1 hectare. The construction of airfields, unless included in schedule 1 and where the works exceed 1 hectare or involves the extension of a runway. Construction of harbours and port installations including fishing harbours, unless included in Schedule 1, and where it exceeds 1 hectare. Inland-waterway construction not included in Schedule 1, canalisation and flood-relief works, dams and other installations designed to hold water or store it on a long-term basis, tramways, elevated and underground railways, suspended lines or similar lines of a particular type, used exclusively or mainly for passenger transport, where the works exceed 1 hectare. Oil and gas pipeline installations (exceeding 7 bar gauge) and pipelines for the transport of carbon dioxide streams for the purposes of geological storage, unless included in Schedule 1, and the installations of long-distance aqueducts where the works exceed 1 hectare. All coastal work to combat erosion and maritime works capable of altering the coast through the construction, for example, of dykes, moles, jetties and other sea defence works, excluding the maintenance and reconstruction of such works. Groundwater abstraction and artificial groundwater recharge schemes not included in Schedule 1, and works for the transfer of water resources between river basins not included in Schedule 1 where the area of works exceeds 1 hectare. Finally, motorway service areas, where the development exceeds 0.5 hectares.

11 Other projects

Permanent racing and test tracks for motorised vehicles where the development exceeds 1 hectare. Installations for the disposal of waste, unless included in Schedule 1, where the disposal is by incineration, or the site exceeds 0.5 hectares or the installation is sited within 100 metres of any controlled water. Waste-water treatment plants, unless included within schedule 1, where the development exceeds 1,000 square metres. Sludge deposition sites and scrap iron storage sites (including scrap vehicles) where the area of deposit or storage exceeds 0.5 hectares or the deposit or storage is within 100 metres of controlled water. Test benches for engines, turbines or reactors, installations for the manufacture of artificial mineral fibres, installations for the recovery or destruction of explosive substances and knackers' yards where the floorspace exceeds 1,000 square metres.

12. Tourism and leisure

Ski-runs, ski-lifts and cable-cars and associated developments where the area of works exceeds 1 hectare or the height of any building or structure exceeds 15 metres. Marinas where the enclosed water surface exceeds 1,000 square metres. Holiday villages and hotel complexes outside urban areas and associated developments or theme parks where the area of development exceeds 0.5 hectares. Permanent camp sites and caravan sites and golf courses and associated developments where the development area exceeds 1 hectare.

13. Changes and extensions

Paragraph 13 covers any change to or extension of development of a description listed in Schedule 1, other than a change or extension falling within paragraph 24 of that Schedule, where that development is already authorised, executed or in the process of being executed. Also, any change to or extension of development of a description listed in paragraphs 1 to 12 of column 1 of the Schedule 2 list, where that development is already authorised, executed or in the process of being executed. Finally, development of a description mentioned in Schedule 1 undertaken exclusively or mainly for the development and testing of new methods or products and not used for more than two years.[43] In relation to paragraph 13 the question whether it is only the change or extension that needed to be considered, or the whole project taking into account the change in the case of *R (on the application of Baker) v Bath and North East Somerset Council* [2009] All ER (D) 169 (Jul) where Collins J held that it was the impact of the whole proposal, and not just the change that had to be considered.

If the Secretary of State or planning authority decide that a Schedule 2 development is proposed within a sensitive area, or at a level at or exceeding the threshold, the next question is whether or not the development is likely to have a significant effect on the environment. This is called a 'screening direction' when made by the Secretary of State or a 'screening opinion' when made by a planning authority.[44]

A prospective developer is also entitled to request a screening opinion from the local planning authority.[45] Such screening request must be accompanied by a plan, a description of the development, a description of the location of the development including environmentally sensitive areas, a description of aspects of the environment likely to be significantly affected and such other information or representations as the developer might wish to make including mitigation that could be applied.

Regulation 18 and Schedule 4 of the EIA Regs sets out the information required to be submitted as part of the environmental statement. A planning authority must adopt a screening position within three weeks of the date of receipt of a request, or may take such longer period not exceeding 90 days as might be agreed. The local authority may, in exceptional circumstances, extend that period.

---

[43] Paragraph 13 Changes and extensions includes quite specific provisons and the legislation should be consulted if the initial criteria are met.

[44] Reg 2 EIA 2017 Regulations SI 2017/571.

[45] Reg 6 EIA 2017 Regulations SI 2017/571.

Where a planning authority either fails to adopt a screening position within the relevant time or adopts an opinion to the effect that the development is an EIA development, the Secretary of State can be asked to provide a screening direction.[46] The Secretary of State is also entitled to request an EIA assessment when an application has been referred to them pursuant to Section 77 of the Town and Country Planning Act 1990, or on appeal pursuant to Section 78.

Factors to be taken into account are set out in Schedule 3 of the EIA Regulations. They include the following:

Characteristics of development

1 The characteristics of development must be considered with particular regard to—

(a) the size and design of the whole development;

(b) cumulation with other existing development and/or approved development;

(c) the use of natural resources, in particular land, soil, water and biodiversity;

(d) the production of waste;

(e) pollution and nuisances;

(f) the risk of major accidents and/or disasters relevant to the development concerned, including those caused by climate change, in accordance with scientific knowledge;

(g) the risks to human health (for example, due to water contamination or air pollution).

---

46 Regs 6(10) and 7 EIA 2017 Regulations SI 2017/571.

Location of development

2(1) The environmental sensitivity of geographical areas likely to be affected by development must be considered, with particular regard, to—

(a) the existing and approved land use;

(b) the relative abundance, availability, quality and regenerative capacity of natural resources (including soil, land, water and biodiversity) in the area and its underground;

(c) the absorption capacity of the natural environment, paying particular attention to the following areas—

(i) wetlands, riparian areas, river mouths;

(ii) coastal zones and the marine environment;

(iii) mountain and forest areas;

(iv) nature reserves and parks;

(v) European sites and other areas classified or protected under national legislation;

(vi) areas in which there has already been a failure to meet the environmental quality standards, laid down in Union legislation and relevant to the project, or in which it is considered that there is such a failure;

(vii) densely populated areas;

(viii) landscapes and sites of historical, cultural or archaeological significance.

Types and characteristics of the potential impact

3 The likely significant effects of the development on the environment must be considered in relation to criteria set out in paragraphs 1 and 2 above, with regard to the impact of the development on the factors specified in regulation 4(2), taking into account—

(a) the magnitude and spatial extent of the impact (for example geographical area and size of the population likely to be affected);

(b) the nature of the impact;

(c) the transboundary nature of the impact;

(d) the intensity and complexity of the impact;

(e) the probability of the impact;

(f) the expected onset, duration, frequency and reversibility of the impact;

(g) the cumulation of the impact with the impact of other existing and/or approved development;

(h) the possibility of effectively reducing the impact.

To consider whether a development is likely to have a significant effect, the following approach was adopted by the Court of Appeal in *R (on the application of Loader) v Secretary of State for Communities and Local Government and others.*[47] Pill LJ found:

---

[47] *R (on the application of Loader) v Secretary of State for Communities and Local Government and others* [2012] EWCA Civ 869

> *What emerges is that the test to be applied is "Is this project likely to have significant effects on the environment?" That is clear from European and national authority, including the Commission Guidance at B3.4.1. The criteria to be applied are set out in the Regulations and judgment is to be exercised by planning authorities focusing on the circumstances of the particular case.*

Additionally,

> *The decision maker must have regard to the precautionary principle and to the degree of uncertainty, as to environmental impact, at the date of the decision. Depending on the information available, the decision maker may or may not be able to make a judgment as to the likelihood of significant effects on the environment. There may be cases where the uncertainties are such that a negative decision cannot be taken. Subject to that, proposals for ameliorative or remedial measures may be taken into account by the decision maker.'*

The meaning of 'is likely to have' was considered in *R (Bateman) v South Cambridgeshire DC and another*[48] to mean *'something more than a bare possibility is probably required, though any serious possibility would suffice.'*

The question of the detail required at the screening stage has been considered in various cases. In *Hockley v Essex County Council and another*[49] Lindblom J stated, *'There has to be a sensible limit to what a screening decision-maker is expected to do'*, and in *Mackman v SSCLG*[50] it was held in the High Court that a screening direction was a preliminary

48 *R (Bateman) v South Cambridgeshire DC and another* [2011] EWCA Civ 157

49 *Hockley v Essex County Council and another* [2013] EWHC 4051 (Admin)

50 *Mackman v SSCLG* [2013] EWHC 3396 (The citation given is for the High Court hearing, which decision was upheld on appeal [2015] EWCA Civ 716.

assessment rather than an examination paper expected to contain a record of each and every issue.

There is a requirement for consultation with relevant statutory consultees. In relation to habitats, the consultees are likely to include Natural England, the Environment Agency, the Marine Management Organisation, National Parks Authorities amongst other possible candidates depending on the circumstances of the application.[51]

The Planning Practice Guidance for EIA indicates that reasonably foreseeable cumulative effects can be assessed: *'Each application (or request for a screening opinion) should be considered on its own merits. There are occasions, however, when other existing or approved development may be relevant in determining whether significant effects are likely as a consequence of a proposed development. The local planning authorities should always have regard to the possible cumulative effects arising from any existing or approved development.'*[52] Often the question of cumulative effects will arise in the context of other regulation, such as the impact of intensive farming on river water quality and nitrate vulnerable zones.[53]

Should a decision or opinion be reached that an environmental impact assessment is required, subject to the Secretary of State's powers to make directions, an environmental statement will need to be prepared and submitted with the planning application.

---

[51] The Town and Country Planning (Development Management Procedure) (England) Order 2015.

[52] Paragraph: 024 Reference ID: 4-024-20170728.

[53] Apart from affecting safe drinking water World Health Organisation limits, such projects can cause eutrophication of surface waters and estuaries, acidification and eutrophication of upland waters and impact groundwater dependant ecosystems.

It is possible for a developer to submit a planning application together with what it terms an environmental statement[54], in which case the planning authority must treat the application as an EIA application and does not need to go through the screening process.

Submission of an Environmental Impact Assessment Application

An environment statement must be prepared by 'competent experts' whose expertise or qualification must be set out by the applicant.

It should, if there has been a scoping opinion or direction, be based upon the most recent version issued. It must include the information reasonably required for reaching a reasoned conclusion on the significant effects of the development on the environment taking into account current knowledge and methods of assessment and must be prepared, taking into account the results of any relevant UK environmental assessment, which are reasonably available to the person preparing the environmental statement, with a view to avoid duplication of assessment.[55]

An applicant submitting an EIA application to a planning authority must provide an additional copy to be submitted to the Secretary of State by the planning authority within 14 days. The planning authority is also entitled to request additional copies to be supplied to the statutory consultees. The planning authority is also required to notify 'any particular person who is or is likely to be affected.' The planning authority must not determine the application until the expiry of 30 days from the last date on which a copy of the statement was served to permit time for consultation.[56] If an EIA application is submitted to the

54 Reg 18 EIA Regulations 2017 SI 2017/571

55 Reg 18(4) EIA Regulations 2017 SI 2017/571

56 Reg 19 EIA Regulations 2017 SI 2017/571

Secretary of State, they have a duty to supply a copy to the planning authority, and otherwise consult with the relevant bodies.[57]

An applicant has duties to publicise the application, in addition to the local planning authorities' duty to publicise a planning application. The duty on the applicant includes publicity in a local newspaper in a prescribed form, placing a notice on the land, and taking reasonable steps to inform persons who are likely to have an interest in the application.[58]

The planning authority and Secretary of State have the power to request additional information should it be necessary to satisfy the requirements in relation to the content of the Environment Statement such as to enable the decision maker to reach a reasoned decision.

The Secretary of State additionally has a duty to consider whether any proposed development is likely to have significant effects upon any country that has ratified the UN Convention on the Environmental Impact Assessment in a Transboundary Context. (the 'ESPOO Convention'). This includes all neighbouring countries to England and while relevant to a very small number of proposals, by their nature many will be controversial.

In accordance with the ESPOO convention, the Secretary of State must send information about the development to the government of the affected country, and invite them to participate in the consultation procedures, determining with them a reasonable timescale to allow them to do so. In such a case, the Secretary of State may direct[59] planning permission may not be granted until the end of such time as may be necessary for consultations with that government.

57 Reg 22 EIA Regulations 2017 SI 2017/571

58 Reg 20 EIA Regulations 2017 SI 2017/571

59 Reg 31 of the Town and Country (Development Management Procedure)(England) Order 2015.

By the nature of EIA applications, there can often be an overlap as between the EIA Regulations and the assessment provisions of the Conservation of Habitats and Species Regulations 2017 (see later chapter). Regulation 27 of the EIA Regulations stipulates that where in relation to EIA development there is, in addition to the requirement for an EIA to be carried out in accordance with these Regulations, also a requirement to carry out a Habitats Regulation Assessment, the relevant planning authority or the Secretary of State, as the case may be, must, where appropriate, ensure that the Habitats Regulation Assessment and the EIA are co-ordinated.

The Effect of an EIA on the Planning Decision

Regulation 26 of the EIA regulations sets out the role of an EIA assessment in the planning process.

> *(1) When determining an application or appeal in relation to which an environmental statement has been submitted, the relevant planning authority, the Secretary of State or an inspector, as the case may be, must—*
>
> > *(a) examine the environmental information;*
> >
> > *(b) reach a reasoned conclusion on the significant effects of the proposed development on the environment, taking into account the examination referred to in sub-paragraph (a) and, where appropriate, their own supplementary examination;*
> >
> > *(c) integrate that conclusion into the decision as to whether planning permission or subsequent consent is to be granted; and*
> >
> > *(d) if planning permission or subsequent consent is to be granted, consider whether it is appropriate to impose monitoring measures.*

Obligations in relation to mitigation and monitoring would normally be addressed by conditioning any planning approval using sections 70, 72, 73, 73A and Schedule 5 of the TCPA 1990[60], or through the use of planning obligations using Section 106 of the TCPA 1990.

There is a duty on a local planning authority in granting planning permission for a project subject to EIA to give reasons for granting the permission. The reasons need to amount to an adequate explanation of the ultimate decision taken and, if accepted, a well-reasoned officers' report setting out the relevant background material and policies with a reasoned conclusion would be sufficient.[61]

In relation to planning development, the EIA process can be seen as a significant material consideration in the decision-making process of whether or not to grant a planning permission. If relevant it can act as an important protection in relation to habitats and biodiversity. It is not, however, necessarily determinative of the application that will involve balancing many different issues.

A local planning authority has 16 weeks to make decision in relation to an EIA application.[62] This period can be extended by written agreement between the applicant and planning authority.

What is the position if there has been a failure to comply with the EIA requirements? A series of cases has culminated in the Supreme Court case of *R (on the application of Champion) v North Norfolk District Council.*[63] Champion confirmed that it was 'well settled' that even where there is a

---

60 Or Sections 77, 79, 177 and Schedule 6 of the TCPA 1990 if exercised by the Secretary of State.

61 R (on the application of CPRE Kent) v Dover District Council and another [2018] 2 All ER 121.

62 Reg 68 EIA Regulations 2017 SI 2017/571.

63 R (on the application of Champion) v North Norfolk District Council [2015] UKSC 52

breach of EIA Regulations, that a court retained a discretion as to whether to refuse relief. Account should be taken as to the seriousness of the defect, and the extent to which it deprived the public concerned of allowing their access to information and participation in the decision-making. The Court determined that on the facts of that case, that there was nothing to suggest that the local authorities' decision would have been different had the investigations and consultations taken place within the framework of the EIA Regulations and declined to quash the decision.

CHAPTER THREE

MARINE WORKS – ENVIRONMENTAL IMPACT ASSESSMENT

The Marine Works (Environmental Impact Assessment) Regulations 2007 ('Marine EIA Regulations') is applicable to any regulated activity, which in turn means any activity for which regulatory approval is required under:

A licence under Part 2 of the Food and Environment Protection Act 1985

(Including the licencing the depositing of substances at sea from a ship, container or structure on land designed for depositing at sea and the loading of substances for deposit),

A marine licence under Part 4 of the Marine and Coastal Act 2009 (the Marine Management Organisation power to grant marine licences for licensable activities such as dredging, removal or depositing materials, constructing altering or improvement works in or over the sea or on the seabed and scuttling ships.),

An approval for harbour works under any local Act;

a local Act read together with a notice given and published under Section 9 of the Harbours Transfer Act 1862 (Powers of the Admiralty to retain authority over ports);

any order under Sections 14 or 16 of the Harbours Act 1964 (Minister's powers on application to secure harbour efficiency, improvements and construction)

In the case of Marine Environmental Impact Assessment, the appropriate authority is either the Secretary of State or the Marine Management Organisation (MMO).[64] The regulator is *the person responsible for considering an application for a regulatory approval and may be, by way of examples, a port authority, the Environment Agency or the MMO.*

Where an EIA is required, *unless the appropriate authority has given EIA consent, the regulator must not grant a regulatory approval in respect of the regulated activity and the applicant must not commence the regulated activity.*[65]

It can be seen that there is a potential for overlap as between the areas covered by the EIA Regulations and the Marine EIA Regulations. While there are significant similarities within the core provisions, care needs to be taken in applications straddling both regulations to ensure that all relevant material, regulations and treaties are considered.

In relation to determining any authorisations in the marine environment that include granting, varying, revocation or placing conditions on a permit issued pursuant to the Environmental Permitting (England and Wales) Regulations 2016 or licensing the abstraction or impoundment under the Water Resources Act 1991, there are duties on the Secretary of State and Environment Agency to ensure compliance with the requirements of the Water Framework Directive[66], the Groundwater Directive[67] and the Environmental Quality Standards Directive.[68] There are additional duties to prevent the deterioration of the surface water

64 Reg 2 Marine Works (Environmental Impact Assessment) Regulations 2007 (SI 2007/1518)

65 Reg 4 Marine Works (Environmental Impact Assessment) Regulations 2007 (SI 2007/1518)

66 Water Framework Directive 2000/60/EC.

67 Groundwater Directive 2006/118/EEC.

68 Environmental Quality Standards Directive 2008/105/EC.

status or groundwater status of a body of water and to otherwise support the achievement of the environmental objectives set for a body of water.[69]

By way of example, in relation to the importance of the Water Framework Directive and decision-making in relation to applications the European Court of Justice ruled in *Case C-461/13 Bund fur Umwelt und Naturschutz Deutschland* that this obligation:

(i) "*…must be interpreted as meaning that the Member States are required — unless a derogation is granted — to refuse authorisation for an individual project where it may cause a deterioration of the status of a body of surface water or where it jeopardises the attainment of good surface water status or of good ecological potential and good surface water chemical status by the date laid down by the directive.*";

and

(ii) "*…must be interpreted as meaning that there is deterioration as soon as the status of at least one of the quality elements, within the meaning of Annex V to the directive, falls by one class, even if that fall does not result in a fall in classification of the body of surface water as a whole. However, if the quality element concerned, within the meaning of that annex, is already in the lowest class, any deterioration of that element constitutes a 'deterioration of the status' of a body of surface water, within the meaning of Article 4(1)(a)(i).*"

The 'environmental objectives,' in relation to a river basin district or body of water, means the objectives set under regulation 12 in accordance with regulation 13. The objectives set out in Regulation 13 of the Water

69 Water Environment (Water Framework Directive)(England and Wales) Regulations 2017 (SI 2017/407)

Environment (Water Framework Directive) (England and Wales) Regulations 2017 are:

> *(2) For surface water bodies, the objectives are to—*
>
> > *(a) prevent deterioration of the status of each body of surface water;*
> >
> > *(b) protect, enhance and restore each body of surface water (other than an artificial or heavily modified water body) with the aim of achieving good ecological status and (subject to paragraph (3)) good surface water chemical status, if not already achieved, by 22nd December 2021;*
> >
> > *(c) protect and enhance each artificial or heavily modified water body with the aim of achieving good ecological potential and (subject to paragraph (3)) good surface water chemical status, if not already achieved, by 22nd December 2021;*
> >
> > *(d) aim progressively to reduce pollution from priority substances and aim to cease or phase out emissions, discharges and losses of priority hazardous substances.*
>
> *(3) The objectives in paragraph (2)(b) and (c) are to be read as though they referred to achieving good surface water chemical status—*
>
> > *(a) in relation to substances 2, 5, 15, 20, 22, 23 and 28 in the table of priority substances, by 22nd December 2021;*[70]

---

[70] These are a list of substances set out in the Water Framework and Environmental Quality Standards Directives, for example, certain polyaromatic hydrocarbons, hydrocarbons, as well as elements like lead, nickel, mercury and substances like cyanide.

(b) in relation to substances 34 to 45 in the table of priority substances, by 22nd December 2027.

(4) For shellfish water protected areas, in addition to the objectives under paragraph (2) for the surface water bodies in which they are located, the objectives are such objectives as are necessary or desirable to improve or protect the shellfish water protected area in order to support shellfish life and growth and to contribute to the high quality of shellfish products suitable for human consumption as the appropriate authority may direct.

(5) For groundwater bodies, the objectives are to—

(a) prevent deterioration of the status of each body of groundwater;

(b) prevent or limit the input of pollutants into groundwater;

(c) protect, enhance and restore each body of groundwater, and ensure a balance between abstraction and recharge of groundwater, with the aim of achieving good groundwater chemical status and good groundwater quantitative status, if not already achieved, by 22nd December 2021;

(d) reverse any significant and sustained upward trend in the concentration of any pollutant resulting from the impact of human activity in order to progressively reduce pollution of groundwater.

In a similar manner to the EIA Regulations, the Marine EIA Regulations list Schedule A1 projects for which an EIA is a mandatory requirement[71] and Schedule A2 projects that the appropriate authority (the MMO or

71 Reg 7 Marine Works (Environmental Impact Assessment) Regulations 2007 (SI 2007/1518)

Secretary of State) determines is required *if it concludes that the project in question is likely, because of its size, nature or location, to have significant effects on the environment.*[72] *An EIA can also be carried out by agreement between the applicant and appropriate authority.*

Schedule A1 lists 31 projects that include crude oil refineries, nuclear power stations and trading ports able to take vessels in excess of 1,350 tonnes.

Schedule A2 lists 90 separate projects including the extraction of minerals by dredging, shipyards, intensive fish farming and reclamation from the sea.

The criteria to be used to assess whether Schedule A2 projects are likely to have significant effects on the environment are set out in Schedule 1 of the Marine EIA Regulations:

> *The Characteristics of the project*
>
> *1 The characteristics of the project, with particular regard to—*
>
> *(a) the size and design of the whole project;*
>
> *(b) cumulation with other existing or approved projects;*
>
> *(c) the use of natural resources, in particular land, soil, water and biodiversity;*
>
> *(d) the production of waste;*
>
> *(e) pollution and nuisances;*
>
> *(f) the risk of major accidents or disasters which are relevant to the project concerned, including those caused*

72 Reg 8 Marine Works (Environmental Impact Assessment) Regulations 2007 (SI 2007/1518)

by climate change, in accordance with scientific knowledge; and

(g) the risks to human health (for example due to water contamination or air pollution).

Location of the project

2 *The environmental sensitivity of geographical areas likely to be affected by the project, with particular regard to—*

(a) the existing and approved land use;

(b) the relative abundance, availability, quality and regenerative capacity of natural resources (including soil, land, water and biodiversity) in the area and below ground in that area;

(c) the absorption capacity of the natural environment, paying particular attention to the following areas—

(i) wetlands, riparian areas, river mouths;

(ii) coastal zones and the marine environment;

(iii) mountain and forest areas;

(iv) nature reserves and parks;

(v) areas classified or protected under national legislation, Natura 2000 areas designated or classified by member States pursuant to the Habitats Directive or the Wild Birds Directive;

(vi) areas in which there has already been a failure to meet the environmental quality standards laid down in EU legislation [as it applied in the

United Kingdom immediately prior to exit day, or in retained EU law] and relevant to the project, or in which it is considered that there is such a failure;

(vii) densely populated areas; and

(viii) landscapes and sites of historical, cultural or archaeological significance.

Types and characteristics of the potential impact

3 The likely significant effects of projects on the environment in relation to the matters set out in paragraphs 1 and 2, with regard to the impact of the project on the factors specified in regulation 21A(2)(a) to (e) and with regard to—

(a) the magnitude and spatial extent of the impact (for example the geographical area and the size of the population likely to be affected);

(b) the nature of the impact;

(c) the transboundary nature of the impact;

(d) the intensity and complexity of the impact;

(e) the probability of the impact;

(f) the expected onset, duration, frequency and reversibility of the impact;

(g) the cumulation of the impact with the impact of other existing or approved projects;

(h) the possibility of effectively reducing the impact.

An Environmental Impact Assessment is not required in relation to national defence projects if the Secretary of State so directs, or in response to a civil emergency if the appropriate authority so directs. There are also exceptions to the need to carry out an EIA for a number of criteria including circumstances where an EIA is being carried out by another consenting authority,[73] or where the Secretary of State directs one is not required in exceptional circumstances in accordance with Article 2(4) of the EIA Directive.

A prospective applicant is entitled to request a screening opinion from the appropriate authority at any time before they apply for approval in relation to a regulated activity from the regulator. Should an application then be submitted to the regulator, the regulator must not deal with the application until after the appropriate authority has given its screening opinion. *If an applicant makes an application for a regulatory approval in relation to a regulated activity without having requested a screening opinion, and the regulator considers that the regulated activity is or may be one in relation to which an environmental impact assessment is required, the regulator must direct the applicant to request a screening opinion from the appropriate authority, and, must not deal with the application until after the appropriate authority has given its screening opinion.*[74]

Applying for Regulatory Approval

When applying for regulatory approval of a regulated activity an application should be prepared by competent persons and the application must be accompanied by a statement from the applicant outlining the relevant experience or qualifications of such persons.

The application submitted to the regulator should include *a chart or map (or both) sufficient to identify where the regulated activity would be carried*

[73] Reg 10 Marine Works (Environmental Impact Assessment) Regulations 2007 (SI 2007/1518)

[74] Reg 11 Marine Works (Environmental Impact Assessment) Regulations 2007 (SI 2007/1518)

out and the extent of any operations which it would involve, a description (including a plan) of the nature of the project, identifying the regulated activity to be carried out in the course of that project, a statement of the working methods to be used in the course of the project and in carrying out the regulated activity, an environmental statement in respect of the project and a copy of any environmental statement in respect of the project provided or to be provided to any other consenting authority.

An environmental statement must be in writing and *include, at least, a description of the project and the regulated activity, comprising information on the site, design, size and other relevant features of the project. The statement must also include:*

- *details of the regulated activity,*

- *a description of the likely significant effects of the project and the regulated activity on the environment,*

- *a description of the features of the project and the regulated activity or the measures envisaged in order to avoid, prevent or reduce and, if possible, offset likely significant adverse effects on the environment,*

- a *description of the reasonable alternatives studied by the applicant which are relevant to the project and its specific characteristics,*

- *and an indication of the main reasons for the option chosen, taking into account the effects of the project on the environment,*

- *a non-technical summary of the information referred to above and,*

- *any additional information specified in Schedule 3 of the Marine EIA Regulations.*

The environmental statement must be *relevant to the specific characteristics of a particular project or type of project and to the environmental features likely to be affected.*

> *Where a scoping opinion has been given it should be based on the most recent scoping opinion given so far as the project remains materially the same as the project which was subject to that opinion.*

The environmental statement should *include the information reasonably required for reaching a conclusion about the significant effects of the project on the environment, taking into account current knowledge and methods of assessment. If there is a failure to provide sufficient information, if the appropriate authority reasonably considers that it requires additional information to enable it to properly consider the likely significant effects of the project arising from the regulated activity, and that the applicant is able to supply it, the appropriate authority can write to request it. A failure to provide that information can result in the appropriate authority deeming the application as being withdrawn* or they *may direct the relevant regulator to do so.*[75]

> *The environmental statement can, with a view to avoiding duplication of assessments, be prepared taking into account the results of any relevant UK environmental assessment which are reasonably available to the applicant.*
>
> *Schedule 3 of the Marine EIA Regulations* fully *sets out the information to be included in an Environmental Statement:*
>
> *1 A description of the project and of the regulated activity, including in particular:*

[75] Reg 14 Marine Works (Environmental Impact Assessment) Regulations 2007 (SI 2007/1518)

(a) *a description of the location of the project and the regulated activity;*

(b) *a description of the physical characteristics of the whole project and regulated activity, including where relevant, requisite demolition works, and the land-use requirements during the construction and operational phases;*

(c) *a description of the main characteristics of the operational phase of the project and the regulated activity (in particular any production process): for instance, energy demand and energy used, the nature and quantity of the materials and natural resources (including water, land, soil and biodiversity) used;*

(d) *an estimate, by type and quantity, of expected residues and emissions (such as water, air, soil and subsoil pollution, noise, vibration, light, heat, radiation and quantities and types of waste produced during the construction and operation phases) resulting from the operation of the proposed project and the regulated activity.*

2 *A description of the reasonable alternatives (for example in terms of project design, technology, location, size and scale) studied by the applicant, which are relevant to the proposed project, the regulated activity and their specific characteristics, and an indication of the main reasons for selecting the chosen option, including a comparison of the environmental effects.*

3 *A description of the relevant aspects of the current state of the environment (baseline scenario), and an outline of the likely evolution thereof without implementation of the project, as far as natural changes from the baseline scenario can be assessed with reasonable effort on the basis of the availability of environmental information and scientific knowledge.*

4 *A description of the factors specified in regulation 21A(2)(a) to (e) likely to be significantly affected by the project and the regulated activity: population, human health, biodiversity (for example, fauna and flora), land (for example, land take), soil (for example, organic matter, erosion, compaction, sealing), water (for example, hydromorphological changes, quantity and quality), air, climate (for example, greenhouse gas emissions, impacts relevant to adaptation), material assets, cultural heritage, including architectural and archaeological aspects, and landscape.*

5 *A description of the likely significant effects of the project and the regulated activity on the environment resulting from, inter alia—*

(a) the construction and existence of the project and the regulated activity, including, where relevant, demolition works;

(b) the use of natural resources, in particular land, soil, water and biodiversity, considering as far as possible the sustainable availability of these resources;

(c) the emission of pollutants, noise, vibration, light, heat and radiation, the creation of nuisances, and the disposal and recovery of waste;

(d) the risks to human health, cultural heritage or the environment (for example, due to accidents or disasters);

(e) the cumulation of effects with other existing or approved projects, taking into account any existing environmental problems relating to areas of particular environmental importance likely to be affected or the use of natural resources;

(f) the impact of the project on climate (for example, the nature and magnitude of greenhouse gas emissions) and the vulnerability of the project to climate change;

(g) the technologies and the substances used.

6 *The description of the likely significant effects on the factors specified in regulation 21A(2)(a) to (e) must cover the direct effects and any indirect, secondary, cumulative, transboundary, short-term, medium-term and long-term, permanent and temporary, positive and negative effects of the project and the regulated activity. This description must take into account the environmental protection objectives [in retained EU law or under the law of any part of the United Kingdom] which are relevant to the project and the regulated activity.*

7 *A description of the forecasting methods or evidence used to identify and assess the significant effects on the environment including details of difficulties (for example, technical deficiencies or lack of knowledge) encountered compiling the required information and the main uncertainties involved.*

8 *A description of the measures envisaged to avoid, prevent, reduce or if possible offset any identified significant adverse effects on the environment and, where appropriate, of any proposed monitoring arrangements (for example, the preparation of a post-project analysis). That description must explain the extent to which significant adverse effects on the environment are avoided, prevented, reduced or offset, and must cover both the construction and operational phases.*

9 *A description of the expected significant adverse effects of the project and the regulated activity on the environment deriving from the vulnerability of the project and the regulated activity to risks of major accidents or disasters which are relevant to the project and the regulated activity concerned. Relevant information*

available and obtained through risk assessments pursuant to retained EU law such as any law that implemented Directive 2012/18/EU of the European Parliament and of the Council on the control of major accident hazards involving dangerous substances, amending and subsequently repealing Council Directive 96/82/EC or Council Directive 2009/71/Euratom establishing a Community framework for the nuclear safety of nuclear installations or UK environmental assessments may be used for this purpose provided that the requirements of any law that implemented the EIA Directive are met. Where appropriate, this description must include measures envisaged to prevent or mitigate the significant adverse effects of such events on the environment and details of the preparedness for and proposed response to such emergencies.

10 A non-technical summary of the information provided under paragraphs 1 to 9.

11 A reference list detailing the sources used for the descriptions and assessments included in the report.

The information supplied in the Environmental Statement must both be accurate and include all relevant material. Regulation 25 of the Marine EIA Regulations makes it a criminal offence to either knowingly or recklessly make a false statement or to intentionally fail to disclose any material particular for the purpose of procuring or obtaining an EIA consent.

In relation to applications made under the Marine EIA Regulations, there is a similar approach to those made under the EIA regulations. There are duties to publicise the application and environmental statement placed on the appropriate authority, that can also direct that publicity is given in newspapers and such other manner as the authority considers appropriate.[76] In relation to public consultation responses Schedule 5 of the EIA Regulations 2007 sets out a procedure for dealing with the results of the consultations, including whether they can be disregarded and if relevant, who the information should be shared with. It also sets out circumstances whereby a local inquiry can be instigated.

There is a duty to consult with relevant consultation bodies, allowing them either 42 days or a longer period as may be agreed between the consultation body and the appropriate authority, to respond. The regulator may not reach a decision until the consultation period has passed.[77]

There is a legal obligation to share information with to consult with European Economic Area (EEA) states where either it comes to the attention of the appropriate authority that a proposed project is likely to have a significant effect on the environment in an EEA state or where an EEA state that is likely to be significantly affected by the project requests.[78]

Where, in respect of a regulated activity, there is a requirement to carry out an environmental impact assessment and an assessment under any law of any part of the United Kingdom that implemented the Habitats Directive or the Wild Birds Directive the appropriate authority must, where appropriate, ensure that the assessments are co-ordinated.

---

[76] Reg 16 Marine Works (Environmental Impact Assessment) Regulations 2007 (SI 2007/1518)

[77] Reg 17 Marine Works (Environmental Impact Assessment) Regulations 2007 (SI 2007/1518)

[78] Regs 18-20 Marine Works (Environmental Impact Assessment) Regulations 2007 (SI 2007/1518)

The Decision

Reg 21A of the Marine EIA Regulations sets out the approach that the appropriate authority should take in assessing the application.

> *(1) The appropriate authority must consider (ensuring that in doing so it has or has access to any expertise it considers necessary)—*
>
> *(a) the environmental statement;*
>
> *(b) any further information provided by the applicant pursuant to a notification under regulation 14(1);*
>
> *(c) the outcome of the process set out in Schedule 5 in relation to any representations received pursuant to the statement referred to in regulation 16(2)(g);*
>
> *(d) any representations in response to consultation made by the consultation bodies pursuant to the letter referred to in regulation 17(1)(a)(iv);*
>
> *(e) the outcome of any consultation of the authorities of... EEA States carried out in accordance with regulation 20; and*
>
> *(f) any features of the project in relation to the regulated activity being carried out, or measures which the applicant proposes to take, which would have the effect of avoiding, preventing, reducing or offsetting any likely significant adverse environmental effects of the regulated activity.*
>
> *(2) Following the consideration required by paragraph (1), the appropriate authority must reach a conclusion about the likely significant effects of the project (including the expected effects deriving from the vulnerability of the project to risks of major accidents or disasters) on—*

> (a) *population and human health;*
>
> (b) *biodiversity, with particular attention to species and habitats protected under any law of any part of the United Kingdom that implemented the Habitats Directive and the Wild Birds Directive;*
>
> (c) *land, soil, water, air and climate;*
>
> (d) *material assets, cultural heritage and the landscape; and*
>
> (e) *the interaction between the factors referred to in sub-paragraphs (a) to (d).*

The Regulation requires that in reaching its decision that the appropriate authority must have regard to the application, to its conclusion under regulation 21A(2) (set out above), whether such conclusion is up-to-date and considering whether monitoring of the significant adverse environmental effects of the regulated activity is appropriate including the addition of conditions to any regulatory approval.

In *Thompson v Marine Management Organisation*[79] a challenge was brought on the basis that the MMO, in issuing a licence, had failed in law to correctly consider an attribute of the subtidal Goodwin Sands that was to be dredged under the terms of the licence. The challenge was brought on the basis that the JNCC guidance in relation to the 'inshore sublittoral sediments' had not been followed. The Judge found that the MMO, in taking and complying with advice from Natural England as the statutory consultee, who had themselves considered the JNCC guidance, had followed the correct approach in law.

In practice, monitoring and conditions attached to approvals have tended to be fixed at the point of consent. There has recently been increasing

---

79 Thompson v Marine Management Organisation [2019] EWHC 2368 (Admin)

pressure to adopt adaptive environmental management plans in long-term consents, such as that attached to the Swansea Bay Tidal Lagoon hydro-electrical project implemented by Natural Resources Wales. Large-scale long-terms projects affecting the marine environment will now often include significant monitoring to identify factors that will affect the marine environment in years to come, such as climate change. By way of example, the varied permit in relation to Hinkley C nuclear power station's operational water discharge activities related to the cooling system, that was determined on 26th July 2023, includes significant monitoring to assess shifting species distribution that is anticipated as a result of climate change. In varying the Hinkley C permit[80], the Environment Agency considered the provisions of the OSPAR Convention that requires Contracting Parties (as the UK is) to apply best available technology and best environmental practice, including, where appropriate, clean technology, in their efforts to prevent and eliminate marine pollution.

Once a licence has been granted, Section 72 of the Marine and Coastal Access Act 2009 provides the MMO with powers to vary, suspend, revoke the licence if there has been any breach of its provisions, if false or misleading material was supplied during the application or there was an omission of relevant material being included in the application, or because of a change of circumstances relating to the environment or human health, an increase in scientific knowledge, in the interests of navigation or for any other reason that appears to the authority to be relevant.

A licensee may apply to transfer a licence to another party. In *R (on the application of Tarian Hafren Severn Shield Cyf) v MMO*[81] it was held that

---

80 Permit number EPR/HP3228XT.

81 R (on the application of Tarian Hafren Severn Shield Cyf) v MMO [2022] EWHC 683 (Admin)

a variation could include the addition of new activities (in that case a dredging licence being modified to include disposal of material).

Marine Planning

A significant development in recent years has been the publication of marine plans in accordance with Sections 49, 50 and 51 of the Marine and Coastal Access Act 2009. While the Secretary of State is responsible for marine plans, the detailed preparation is delegated to the MMO.

England has 11 marine plan areas, with the North East, East, South, South West and North West each having an inshore and offshore plan. The South East only having an inshore plan. The North West inshore and offshore plan was developed as a single process and only has one plan covering both areas. The inshore plans govern the 12 mile limit while the offshore areas cover areas up to the Exclusive Economic Zone[82] limit that can extend up to 200 miles (this is obviously reduced where neighbouring states have competing interests).

In 2011 the four UK Governments published the Marine Policy Statement (MPS), that set out the framework for the development of Marine Plans and decision taking on matters affecting the marine environment. The MPS provides high-level policy guidance on the approach to be taken to marine issues.

In relation to habitat protection Chapter 2 sets out high level goals including the objective of 'Living within environmental limits' that include the goals that:

[82] The UK Exclusive Economic Zone was created by the Exclusive Economic Zone Order (SI 2013/3161) that was made pursuant to Section 41 of the Marine and Coastal Access Act 2009. In turn this implements agreement reached under the UN Convention on Law of the Sea.

Biodiversity is protected, conserved and where appropriate recovered and loss has been halted.

Healthy marine and coastal habitats occur across their natural range and are able to support strong, biodiverse biological communities and the functioning of healthy, resilient and adaptable marine ecosystems and that,

Our oceans support viable populations of representative, rare, vulnerable, and valued species.

The MPS requires that planning and decision-making is conducted in a manner that is consistent with the requirements under UK and EU legislation[83] and obligations under international law.

Specifically, decisions are to be based on an ecosystem approach.[84] A practical interpretation of the ecosystem approach is set out in regulation 5 of the Marine Strategy Regulations 2010 which transpose the Marine Strategy Framework Directive. An ecosystem-based approach to the management of human activities means an approach which ensures that the collective pressure of human activities is kept within the levels compatible with the achievement of good environmental status; that does not compromise the capacity of marine ecosystems to respond to human-induced changes; and that enables the sustainable use of marine goods and services.

The MPS makes specific reference to key elements of the Marine Strategy Framework Directive, the Water Framework Directive, Habitats and Birds Directives and sets high level goals of maintaining and improving biodiversity, ensuring the quality and occurrence of habitats, that fishing is conducted within safe biological limits, the maintenance of sea floor

83 The Marine Policy Statement wording will have to be read down as affected by European Union (Withdrawal) Act 2018 and other amendments.

84 Para 2.3.1.1 of the Marine Policy Statement.

integrity amongst other objectives. The MPS also refers to construction and operational issues such as noise and air quality issues as well as contamination, the historic environment and seascapes.

Marine plans have been published for English areas with the first being formally adopted in June 2021. The plans follow a formula of setting out a vision, objectives and then specific policies.

An example of a specific policy within the North-East Plan in relation to Marine Protected areas is:[85]

> *Proposals that support the objectives of marine protected areas and the ecological coherence of the marine protected area network will be supported.*
>
> *Proposals that may have adverse impacts on the objectives of marine protected areas must demonstrate that they will, in order of preference:*
>
> *a) avoid*
>
> *b) minimise*
>
> *c) mitigate*
>
> *- adverse impacts, with due regard given to statutory advice on an ecologically coherent network.*

The policy aim states:

> *Marine protected areas in the north east marine plan areas make a significant contribution towards the UK's network of ecologically coherent marine protected areas. NE-MPA-1 encourages and supports proposals for activities that further the conservation objectives of marine protected areas. NE-MPA-1 also ensures proposals take account*

85 NE-MPA-1

of adverse impacts on individual sites and the overall network, protecting important habitats, species and geological features, and enabling the successful and continued management of these sites.

Proposals that cannot avoid, minimise or mitigate adverse impacts should not be supported.

All of the plans contain biodiversity net gain objectives. The question how that would practically be implemented is under consideration under the description of 'marine net gain'.[86] DEFRA have suggested that the 'net gain' provisions will sit completely separately to existing requirements for environmental protection.

What is the effect of the Marine Policy Statement and Marine Plans? Section 58 Marine and Coastal Access Act 2009 sets out their application:

58 Decisions affected by marine policy documents

(1) A public authority must take any authorisation or enforcement decision in accordance with the appropriate marine policy documents, unless relevant considerations indicate otherwise.

(2) If a public authority takes an authorisation or enforcement decision otherwise than in accordance with the appropriate marine policy documents, the public authority must state its reasons.

(3) A public authority must have regard to the appropriate marine policy documents in taking any decision—

[86] As of the summer of 2023, the DEFRA have concluded a consultation and publication of their proposals is expected soon.

(a) *which relates to the exercise of any function capable of affecting the whole or any part of the UK marine area, but*

(b) *which is not an authorisation or enforcement decision.*

(4) *An "authorisation or enforcement decision" is any of the following—*

(a) *the determination of any application (whenever made) for authorisation of the doing of any act which affects or might affect the whole or any part of the UK marine area,*

(b) *any decision relating to any conditions of such an authorisation,*

(c) *any decision about extension, replacement, variation, revocation or withdrawal of any such authorisation or any such conditions (whenever granted or imposed),*

(d) *any decision relating to the enforcement of any such authorisation or any such conditions,*

(e) *any decision relating to the enforcement of any prohibition or restriction (whenever imposed) on the doing of any act, or of any act of any description, falling within paragraph (a),*

but does not include any decision on an application for an order granting development consent under the Planning Act 2008 (c. 29) (in relation to which subsection (3) has effect accordingly).

(5) *In section 104(2) of the Planning Act 2008 (matters to which Panel or Council must have regard in deciding application for order granting development consent) after paragraph (a) insert—*

> *"(aa) the appropriate marine policy documents (if any), determined in accordance with section 59 of the Marine and Coastal Access Act 2009;".*

It follows that the MPS and Marine Plans must be followed unless relevant considerations indicate otherwise. If there is departure from either policy, it is incumbent on the decision maker to state its reasons for doing so.

CHAPTER FOUR

GENERAL BIODIVERSITY DUTY

The Natural Environment and Rural Communities Act 2006 ('NERC 2006') was given Royal assent on the 30th March 2006, with its provisions coming into force thereafter. It created Natural England as an entity, and also sought to provide specific statutory protection aimed at the conservation and enhancement of biodiversity and habitats. Following the passage of the Environment Act 2021, which came into force on 1st January 2023, there were substantial amendments to the 'duty' created:

> *Section 40 Duty to conserve and enhance biodiversity*[87]
>
> *(A1) For the purposes of this section "the general biodiversity objective" is the conservation and enhancement of biodiversity in England through the exercise of functions in relation to England.*
>
> *(1) A public authority which has any functions exercisable in relation to England must from time to time consider what action the authority can properly take, consistently with the proper exercise of its functions, to further the general biodiversity objective.*

For cases prior to 1st January 2023 the requirement that the duty applied to decisions on a case-by-case basis was settled. In *R (on the application of Buglife – Invertebrate Conservation Trust) v Thurrock Thames Gateway Development Corporation* [2008] EWHC 475 (Admin) in which Mitting J stated [para 6]:

---

[87] Shown as amended by the Environment Act 2021 that added the requirement 'and enhance'.

> *"Since 1 October 2006 all local planning authorities, amongst other public bodies, are required by Section 40(1) of the Natural Environment and Rural Communities Act 2006 . . . in exercising their functions, to have regard so far as is consistent with the proper exercise of those functions, to the purpose of conserving biodiversity."*[88]

However, since the amendments brought about by the Environment Act 2021, there is a cogent argument that the duty is of a more general nature and that the words 'from time to time' require an authority to review plans, rather than to consider biodiversity issues on a case-by-case basis.[89]

Section 41 of NERC 2006 required the Secretary of State to create a list of the living organisms and types of habitat which in the Secretary of State's opinion are of principal importance for the purpose of conserving or enhancing biodiversity. The list is created in consultation with Natural England.

> *41(3) Without prejudice to section 40(1) and (1A), the Secretary of State must—*
>
> > *(a) take such steps as appear to the Secretary of State to be reasonably practicable to further the conservation of the living organisms and types of habitat included in any list published under this section, or*
> >
> > *(b) promote the taking by others of such steps.*
>
> *(4) The Secretary of State must, in consultation with Natural England—*

---

[88] Another similar case decided before the amendments to Section 40 came into force is R (on the application of Suliman) v Bournemouth, Christchurch and Poole Council [2022] EWHC 1196 (Admin)

[89] This was successfully argued at a permission hearing before HHJ Jarman KC in Hart v South Hams DC on 15/11/2023 (unreported).

(a) *keep under review any list published under this section,*

(b) *make such revisions of any such list as appear to the Secretary of State appropriate, and*

(c) *publish any list so revised as soon as is reasonably practicable after revising it.*

Applying Section 41, the Secretary of State prepared a list of 56 habitats of principal importance in England, as well as a list of 943 species of principal importance in England. The lists have since been updated. The list of species includes both flora and fauna, and lists both terrestrial species (including many commonly recognised species such as the adder, smooth snake and hedgehog) as well as marine species (for example harbour porpoise and killer whales).

In relation to planning application situations where there is no EIA requirement, but where priority habitats and species listed by the Secretary of State are known to be present, there may remain a duty to conserve and enhance such biodiversity and habitat that sits separately to the EIA process. If recent changes remove that as a direct requirement during the decision-making process, it is likely to a material consideration through plans made pursuant to Section 40.

The Section 40 duties, such as they now exist, apply to 'public authorities' and so the obligations contained within Section 40 extend beyond the planning regime. Public authorities include a Minister of the Crown, a public body (including government department, a local authority and a local planning authority, a person holding an office under the Crown created or continued in existence by a general public act or the remuneration of which is paid out of monies provided by Parliament, and also to statutory undertakers.[90]

[90] Section 40(4) NERC 2006

CHAPTER FIVE

THE HABITATS DIRECTIVE AND REGULATIONS

Part 1

Habitats Regulations – The designation and management of the National Site Network

The UK 'National Site Network' comprises areas that are designated as SACs or SPAs under the Conservation of Habitats and Species Regulations 2017 (SI 2017/1012) ('Habitats Regulations 2017') together with areas designated under the Conservation of Offshore Marine Habitats and Species Regulations 2017 (SI 2017/1013)('Offshore Marine Habitats Regulations')[91]. The first part of the following chapter describes the current process for site selection, protected feature designation, and site monitoring and management under the Habitats Regulations. Similar provisions are contained within regulations 7 to 20 of the Offshore Marine Habitats Regulations.

The second part of this chapter considers the operation of the Habitats Regulations when a plan or project is proposed that has the potential to impact on the sites or their features.

[91] The Habitats Regulations (SI 2017/1012) applies to land and inshore areas up to 12 nautical miles. The Offshore Marine Habitats Regulations (SI 2017/1013) apply to sites and beyond the 12 nautical mile limit.

Selection of Sites

Historically the Secretary of State proposed an initial list of sites to be adopted under Regulation 7 of the Conservation (Natural Habitats) Regulations 1994 (SI 1994/2716). The UK as of 2023 has 286 sites covering 5,486,796 hectares which includes both terrestrial and offshore sites. While smaller in number, the geographical area of designated offshore sites is significant.

Special Areas of Conservation (SAC)

Regulation 12 and 13 of the Habitats Regulations 2017 requires the 'appropriate authority'[92] to establish priorities for designating as Special Areas of Conservation such sites as it has determined to be sites of national importance.

The reason underlying the selection of sites is to ensure the conservation of a wide range of rare, threatened or endemic animal and plant species, and the preservation of rare and characteristic habitats.

There is a requirement that the priorities for designating a SAC are established *'in light of–*

> *(a) the importance of the sites for the maintenance at or restoration to a favourable conservation status of*
>
> > *(i) a natural habitat type specified in Annex I to the Habitats Directive; or*
> >
> > *(ii) a species specified in Annex II to the Habitats Directive.'*

---

[92] Regulation 3 defines the appropriate authority as the Secretary of State, and any person exercising the function of the Secretary of State.

The priorities also have to consider the importance of such sites for the coherence of the national site network and the threats of degradation or destruction to which the sites are exposed.

Sites of National Importance

Sites of national importance are sites that contribute significantly to the objective of the maintenance or restoration, at favourable conservation status, in their natural range of the natural habitat types listed in Annex I to the Habitats Directive or the species listed in Annex II to the Directive, and contribute to the maintenance of biological diversity within the Atlantic Biogeographic Region.[93]

For animals that range over wide areas, sites of national importance must correspond to places within the natural range of such species, which present the physical or biological factors essential to their life and reproduction. In the case of wide-ranging aquatic species, sites of national importance must only be implemented where there is a clearly definable area which is distinct in providing the physical and biological factors essential to their life and reproduction.

In determining which sites are of national importance the appropriate authority must make its determination only on the basis of relevant scientific information having regard to the importance of the population of a species or the area of habitat in meeting the objectives for the UK in achieving the priorities set out above.

The process for determining sites of national importance involves applying the criteria in Annex III of the Habitats Directive. The Annex III assessment criteria involves a two-stage process. The Stage I assessment is at a national level to determine the relative importance of

93 The Atlantic Biogeographical Region stretches from the top of the United Kingdom and Ireland, to the northern Portuguese coast. It encompasses all of the UK, Ireland and the Netherlands, and parts of Denmark, Germany, Belgium, France and Spain.

sites of each natural habitat type in Annex I and each species type in Annex II.

In relation to Annex I habitats, the assessment takes into account the degree of representativity of the natural habitat type, the area covered by the natural habitat type in relation to the total area covered by that habitat type within the national territory, the degree of conservation of the structure and functions and its restoration possibilities and a global assessment of the value for the conservation of the natural type concerned.

In relation to Annex II species, the assessment considers the size and density of the population of the species present in relation to the population present within national territory, the degree of conservation of the features of the habitat which are important for the species and its restoration possibilities, the degree of isolation of the population and its natural range, and a global assessment of the value of the site for conservation of the species concerned.

The Stage I process required the state to draw up a list of eligible sites based upon the assessments undertaken. The list therefore shows both the site and the priority natural habitat type and/or species type selected.

Stage II required an assessment of the Community importance[94] of the sites included in the national list, including their contribution to maintaining or re-establishing at favourable conservation status, a natural Annex I habitat or Annex II species and or to the coherence of the National Site Network.

Regulation 12(7) of the Habitats Regulations 2017 was amended following Brexit with the Stage II wording being changed from

---

94 Annex III is to be read with the amendments contained within Regulation 12(7) of the Conservation of Habitats and Species regulations 2017 (SI 2017/1012) following the UK withdrawal from the EU.

'Community importance' to 'National importance.[95]' The stage II assessment requires an assessment of the relative value of the site at national level, the geographic situation of the site in relation to migration routes of Annex II species and whether it belongs to a continuous ecosystem extending beyond the borders of the United Kingdom, the total area of the site, the number of natural habitat types in Annex I and species in Annex II present on the site and the global ecological value of the site.[96]

Within the UK the function of advising the designation of SACs and SPAs has been devolved to the JNCC who co-ordinate the advice to Government from the statutory nature conservation agencies, including Natural England. The JNCC approach has been to separate the process of previous SSSI designations under the Wildlife and Countryside Act 1981 from the Habitats Regulation assessment process. While in some instances there is a clear overlap, the Annex I and Annex II lists do not always encompass SSSI designations, and the selection criteria under Annex III are different to those for a SSSI, for example, SSSIs may not be designated for marine sites below the low water mark.

Where possible the JNCC has, in the SAC and SPA site selection process, replicated SSSI boundaries to simplify administrative arrangements. The JNCC did not apply buffer zones around designated SAC or SPA sites, relying on the measures provided under the planning system to deal with adverse impacts on any qualifying feature of the site(s) arising outside of the site. There is a body of case law that supports the contention that offsite activities that might affect a deterioration in the quality or function of a protected site cannot be ignored. See for example *RSPB v Secretary of State for Communities and Local Government* [2014] EWHC

[95] Conservation of Habitats and Species (Amendment)(EU Exit) Regulations 2019 (SI 2019/579).

[96] All current English site designations were determined while the UK was a member of the EU. There have been a number of new SAC designated sites in Scotland as of 1st February 2022.

1523 (Admin) in which the effects on 'functionally linked land' that is not within an SAC or SPA '*are scrutinised in the same legal framework just as are the direct effects of acts carried out on the protected site itself. That is the only sensible and purposive approach where a species or effect is not confined by a line on a map or boundary fence. This is particularly important where the boundaries of designated sites are drawn tightly as may be the UK practice.*'[97]

Once selected, the suitable site is advised to the UK Government for review, approval and public consultation before it can be added to the register.[98]

The designated national site network site will be listed with details being given that include a site SAC EU Code, the location and local authority responsible for the area and the general site character description.

The Dorset Heaths (Purbeck and Wareham) and Studland Dunes, for example, is listed with a general site character as follows:

- Coastal sand dunes, Sand beaches, Machair (5%)
- Inland water bodies (Standing water, Running water) (4%)
- Bogs, Marshes, Water fringed vegetation, Fens (8%)
- Heath, Scrub, Maquis and Garrigue, Phygrana (79%)
- Dry grassland, Steppes (1%)
- Broad-leaved deciduous woodland (1%)

---

97 Per Ouseley J at para 27.

98 Regulations 16 and 17 of the Conservation of Habitats and Species regulations 2017 (SI 2017/1012).

- Coniferous woodland (1%)
- Mixed woodland (1%)

There follows a list of the Annex I habitats that are a primary reason for the site selection. For the Dorset Heaths site this includes Embryonic shifting dunes, Shifting dunes along the shoreline with Ammophila arenaria ('White dunes'), Atlantic decalcified fixed dunes (* priority feature), Humid dune slacks, Bog Wetlands (* priority feature), etc.

The designation also includes Annex I habitats that are present as a qualifying feature, but not a primary reason for selection of the site. Examples in the Dorset Heaths site include 'Molinia meadows' and 'Alkaline Fens', etc.

The Dorset Heaths site designation includes an Annex II species, the Southern damselfly, which is a primary reason for this site being designated.

Also listed as an Annex II species present as a qualifying feature, but not a primary reason for site selection, are great crested newts.

'Priority features' are habitats or species in danger of disappearance. In relation to the distinction between Annex I habitats and Annex II species that are the 'primary reason' for the site selection, these are listed in order to support the SAC designation of the site and the associated site management and monitoring obligations that follow (see below). All Annex I habitat and II species present, whether the primary reason for site designation or as a qualifying feature, are subject to protection under the Habitats Regulations.

Management of Sites

Once a site has been designated an SAC or SPA, and has therefore become part of the national site network, the Habitats Regulations requires the appropriate authority to manage the site with a view to attaining the conservation its objectives.

Regulation 16A(2) of the Habitats Regulations sets the management objectives of the national site network as follows:

> *(a) to maintain at, or where appropriate restore to, a favourable conservation status in their natural range (so far as it lies in the United Kingdom's territory, and so far as is proportionate)—*
>
> > *(i) the natural habitat types listed in Annex I to the Habitats Directive;*
> >
> > *(ii) the species listed in Annex II to that Directive whose natural range includes any part of the United Kingdom's territory;*
>
> *(b) to contribute, in their area of distribution, to ensuring the survival and reproduction of—*
>
> > *(i) the species of birds listed in Annex I to the new Wild Birds Directive which naturally occur in the United Kingdom's territory;*
> >
> > *(ii) regularly occurring migratory species of birds not listed in that Annex which naturally occur in the United Kingdom's territory;*
>
> *(c) to contribute, to securing compliance with the requirements of Article 2 of the new Wild Birds Directive for the purposes of the duty in regulation 9(1) in relation to the species of birds in paragraph (b) within their area of distribution.*

'Favourable Conservation Status' and 'Conservation Status' are defined in the Habitats Regulations as 'having the meanings given by paragraphs (e) (in relation to habitats) and (i) (in relation to species) of Article 1 of the Habitats Directive.[99] These are:

> *Article 1(e): The conservation status of a natural habitat will be taken as 'favourable' when:*
>
> - *its natural range and areas it covers within that range are stable or increasing, and;*
> - *the specific structure and functions which are necessary for its long-term maintenance exist and are likely to continue to exist for the foreseeable future, and;*
> - *the conservation status of its typical species is favourable as defined in Article 1(i).*
>
> *Article 1(i) The conservation status of a species will be taken as 'favourable' when:*
>
> - *population dynamics data on the species concerned indicate that it is maintaining itself on a long-term basis as a viable component of its natural habitats, and;*
> - *the natural range of the species is neither being reduced nor is likely to be reduced for the foreseeable future, and;*
> - *there is, and will probably continue to be, a sufficiently large habitat to maintain its populations on a long-term basis.*

In addition to site management provisions, National Site Networks, together with SSSIs and Ramsar sites, are subject to 'common standards

[99] Regulation 3 of the Conservation of Habitats and Species regulations 2017 (SI 2017/1012).

monitoring' to measure whether the conservation objectives of the sites have been met. The resulting reports indicate whether the site has achieved favourable, unfavourable-recovering, unfavourable or destroyed (in whole or part) status.

The designation of a site as part of the National Site Network allows the appropriate authority to make nature conservation orders and to serve 'stop notices' in relation to operations on the sites.[100] There is also provision for the implementation of bye-laws in relation to the sites.[101] In 2022, by way of example of the use of these powers, the Marine Management Organisation made *'The Dogger Bank Special Area of Conservation (Specified Area) Bottom Towed Fishing Gear Byelaw 2022.'* This prohibited the use of bottom-towed fishing gear and requires the inboard lash and stow of such equipment within the specified area in order to preserve the SAC features of the Dogger Bank SAC.[102]

---

[100] Regulations 27 and 28 of the Conservation of Habitats and Species regulations 2017 (SI 2017/1012).

[101] Regulation 32 of the Conservation of Habitats and Species regulations 2017 (SI 2017/1012) and Section 129 of the Marine and Coastal Access Act 2009 in relation to Marine Conservation Zones.

[102] The Dogger Bank, in the North Sea, was the location that Greenpeace placed 'art installation' sculptures and granite boulders on the sea bed in an attempt to frustrate bottom towed trawlers. The byelaw followed threatened legal action under the Habitats Directive by Blue Marine Foundation and others that had reached the pre-action protocol letter stage.

Part 2

Plans or Projects affecting the National Site Network

The Operation of Habitats Directive and Conservation of Habitats and Species Regulations 2017

The purpose of the Habitats Directive was, as set out above, to identify and protect habitats and certain species of plants and animals which are particularly vulnerable. The sites chosen for designation are those considered particularly important for that role.

Article 6(3) of the Habitats Directive states:

> *Any plan or project not directly connected with or necessary to the management of the site but likely to have a significant effect thereon, either individually or in combination with other plans or projects, shall be subject to appropriate assessment of its implications for the site in view of the site's conservation objectives. In the light of the conclusions of the assessment of the implications for the site and subject to the provisions of paragraph 4, the competent national authority shall agree to the plan or project only after having ascertained that it will not adversely affect the integrity of the site concerned and, if appropriate, after having obtained the opinion of the general public.*

Article 6(4) states:

> *If, in spite if a negative assessment of the implications for the site and in the absence if alternative solutions, a plan or project must nevertheless be carried out for imperative reasons of overriding public interest, including those of a social or economic nature, the Member State shall take all compensatory measures necessary to ensure that the overall coherence of Natura 2000 is protected. It shall inform the Commission of the compensatory measures adopted.*

Where the site concerned hosts a priority natural habitat type and/or priority species, the only considerations which may be raised are those relating to human health or public safety, to beneficial consequences of primary importance for the environment or, further to an opinion of the Commission, to other imperative reasons of overriding public interest.

Part 6 of The Conservation of Habitats and Species regulations 2017 (SI 2017/1012) provides a framework for decision making when a plan or project is proposed that has the potential to impact on the sites or their features.

Regulation 63 of the Habitats Regulations 2017 states:

63 Assessment of implications for European sites and European offshore marine sites

(1) *A competent authority, before deciding to undertake, or give any consent, permission or other authorisation for, a plan or project which—*

(a) *is likely to have a significant effect on a European site or a European offshore marine site (either alone or in combination with other plans or projects), and*

(b) *is not directly connected with or necessary to the management of that site, must make an appropriate assessment of the implications of the plan or project for that site in view of that site's conservation objectives.*

(2) *A person applying for any such consent, permission or other authorisation must provide such information as the competent authority may reasonably require for the purposes of the assessment or to enable it to determine whether an appropriate assessment is required.*

> *(3) The competent authority must for the purposes of the assessment consult the appropriate nature conservation body and have regard to any representations made by that body within such reasonable time as the authority specifies.*
>
> *(4) It must also, if it considers it appropriate, take the opinion of the general public, and if it does so, it must take such steps for that purpose as it considers appropriate.*
>
> *(5) In the light of the conclusions of the assessment, and subject to regulation 64, the competent authority may agree to the plan or project only after having ascertained that it will not adversely affect the integrity of the European site or the European offshore marine site (as the case may be).*
>
> *(6) In considering whether a plan or project will adversely affect the integrity of the site, the competent authority must have regard to the manner in which it is proposed to be carried out or to any conditions or restrictions subject to which it proposes that the consent, permission or other authorisation should be given.*
>
> ...

Regulation 64 of the Habitats Regulations sets out the Habitat Regulation formulation of Article 6(4) of the Habitats Directive as follows:

> *64 Considerations of overriding public interest*
>
> *(1) If the competent authority is satisfied that, there being no alternative solutions, the plan or project must be carried out for imperative reasons of overriding public interest (which, subject to paragraph (2), may be of a social or economic nature), it may agree to the plan or project notwithstanding a negative assessment of the implications for the European site or the European offshore marine site (as the case may be).*

(2) *Where the site concerned hosts a priority natural habitat type or a priority species, the reasons referred to in paragraph (1) must be either—*

(a) *reasons relating to human health, public safety or beneficial consequences of primary importance to the environment; or*

(b) *any other reasons which the competent authority, having due regard to the opinion of the appropriate authority, considers to be imperative reasons of overriding public interest.*

(3) *Where a competent authority other than the Secretary of State or the Welsh Ministers desires to obtain the opinion of the appropriate authority as to whether reasons are to be considered imperative reasons of overriding public interest, it may submit a written request to the appropriate authority—*

(a) *identifying the matter on which an opinion is sought; and*

(b) *accompanied by any documents or information which may be required.*

(4) *In giving its opinion as to whether the reasons are imperative reasons of overriding public interest, the appropriate authority must have regard to the national interest, and provide its opinion to the competent authority.*

(4A) *Before giving its opinion as to whether the reasons are imperative reasons of overriding public interest, the appropriate authority must consult the following, and have regard to their opinion—*

(a) *the Joint Nature Conservation Committee;*

(b) *where the appropriate authority is the Secretary of State, the devolved administrations;*

> (c) *where the appropriate authority is the Welsh Ministers, the Secretary of State, and the other devolved administrations; and*
>
> (d) *any other person the appropriate authority considers appropriate.*
>
> (5) *Where a competent authority other than the Secretary of State or the Welsh Ministers proposes to agree to a plan or project under this regulation notwithstanding a negative assessment of the implications for the site concerned—*
>
> (a) *it must notify the appropriate authority; and*
>
> (b) *it must not agree to the plan or project before the end of the period of 21 days beginning with the day notified by the appropriate authority as that on which its notification was received, unless the appropriate authority notifies it that it may do so.*
>
> (6) *Without prejudice to any other power, the appropriate authority may give directions to the competent authority in any such case prohibiting it from agreeing to the plan or project, either indefinitely or during such period as may be specified in the direction.*

What is a plan or project?

A plan or project is not defined within the Habitats Directive, nor the Habitats Regulations.[103] There is though, a body of case law that says that the words are to be given a wide meaning. In the *Commission v*

[103] There is a definition of a 'plan or programme' within the Environmental Assessment Plans and Programmes Regulations 2004 (SI 2004/1633)

United Kingdom[104] it was held that water abstraction licences granted pursuant to the Water Resources Act 1991 and land use plans used to develop individual planning decisions are plans or projects within the meaning of the Habitats Regulations.

Further examples of cases include:

Terre Wallone ASBL,[105] in which the European Court of Justice held that the requirement as to whether a 'plan or programme' fell within the environmental assessment provisions of the Strategic Environmental Assessment Directive was whether the plan or programme 'influenced individual projects.' It was not a requirement that the plan or project 'determine the location, nature or size' of the project.

In *R (Boggis) v Natural England,*[106] it was held that the designation of a site as a SSSI that could potentially impact on an SAC, since the effect of the SSSI was to prevent unauthorised coastal erosion protection measures that in turn were said to protect local birds, was not a 'plan or project.'

R (on the application of Berks, Buck and Oxon Wildlife Trust) v Secretary of State for Transport[107] considered whether the Secretary of State's decision to choose a preferred corridor for the proposed Oxford to Cambridge expressway amounted to a 'plan or project', thereby requiring an assessment under the Habitats regulations. The choice of corridor, on the facts, included two mutually exclusive proposed routes and did not preclude other options being considered. In these circumstances, the

---

[104] Commission v United Kingdom [2005] All ER (D) 231 (Oct) and Case C-6/04

[105] Terre Wallone ASBL [2010] ECR I-5611

[106] R (Boggis) v Natural England [2009] EWCA Civ 1061

[107] R (on the application of Berks, Buck and Oxon Wildlife Trust) v Secretary of State for Transport [2019] EWHC 1786 (Admin)

Court held that the decision was not a 'plan' but rather a step being taken in the course of the preparation of a project.

The question whether habitat protection under the Habitats Directive can sit outside of the environmental impact assessment regulations was considered in *Cooperatie Mobilisation for the Environment UA and another v College van gedeputeerde staten van Limburg and another*[108] that is commonly referred to as the 'Dutch Nitrogen' case. The case involved the application of nitrogen containing fertilisers under a Dutch regulation, the 'PAS regulation,' that had been introduced to combat excessive nitrogen deposits. The PAS regulation applied a formulaic calculation to identify permissible deposit levels. The ECJ held that the application of fertilisers for agricultural purposes in the vicinity of a Natura 2000 site could be a 'project' within Article 6(3) of the Habitats Directive, and therefore be subject to Article 6(3) assessment, even though it could not be interpreted as falling within the requirements of the Environmental Impact Assessment Directive (*Directive 2011/92/EU).*

In the case usually abbreviated to '*Waddenzee*' (C-127/02),[109] the underlying facts related to authorisations granted for mechanical cockle fishing in the Netherlands Wadden Sea. It was held that the Habitats Directive was applicable to plans or projects where the activity is carried out periodically for several years on the site concerned and where a licence had to be obtained for it every year. The fact that each new issuance of the licence required an assessment both of the possibility of carrying on that activity and of the site where it may be carried on, did not in itself constitute an obstacle to considering it at the time of each application, as a distinct plan or project within the meaning of the Habitats Directive.

---

108 Cooperatie Mobilisation for the Environment UA and another v College van gedeputeerde staten van Limburg and another C293/17 and C294/17.

109 Landelijke Vereniging tot Behoud van de Waddenzee v Staatssecretaris van Landbouw (Coöperatieve Producentenorganisatie van de Nederlandse Kokkelvisserij UA, intervening) C-127/02.

Is the plan or project directly connected with or necessary to the management of the site? The answer to this question is likely to be a question of fact by reference to the management plan.

Competent and Appropriate Authority

Regulation 7 of the Habitats Regulations defines a 'competent authority' as being any Minister of the Crown, government department, statutory undertaker, public body of any description or person holding public office, and any person exercising any function of the above person/bodies.

An 'appropriate authority' is defined by Regulation 2 as meaning the Secretary of State in relation to England, and any person exercising any function of the Secretary of State.

The Assessment of a Plan or Project – when is an 'Appropriate Assessment' required?

Where a competent authority considers whether to undertake, or give any consent, permission or other authorisation for, a plan or project that is not connected with or necessary to the management of a site, the first question is to determine whether the plan or project is 'likely to have a significant effect'. In *Waddenzee*[110] it was determined:

> *'Art.6(3) of the Habitats Directive must be interpreted as meaning that any plan or project not directly connected with or necessary to the management of the site is to be subject to an appropriate assessment of its implications for the site in view of the site's conservation objectives if it cannot be excluded, on the basis of objective information, that it*

[110] Landelijke Vereniging tot Behoud van de Waddenzee v Staatssecretaris van Landbouw (Coöperatieve Producentenorganisatie van de Nederlandse Kokkelvisserij UA, intervening) C-127/02.

will have a significant effect on that site, either individually or in combination with other plans or projects.'

The question whether a proposal 'can be excluded' at the outset on the basis of objective information is often referred to as 'screening' or 'triggering'. The issue of was considered in the Supreme Court in *R (on the application of Champion) v North Norfolk District Council and another*[111] (a case that considered both EIA assessments and Habitats Regulation assessments) where it was pointed out by Lord Carnwath that:

'The process envisaged by art 6(3) should not be over-complicated. As Richards LJ points out[112]*, in cases where it is not obvious, the competent authority will consider whether the 'trigger' for appropriate assessment is met (and see paras 41–43 of Waddenzee). But this informal threshold decision is not to be confused with a formal 'screening opinion' in the EIA sense. The operative words are those of the Habitats Directive itself.* ***All that is required is that, in a case where the authority has found there to be a risk of significant adverse effects to a protected site, there should be an 'appropriate assessment'.***[113]*'*

The Habitats Directive process is therefore different to that adopted in EIA assessment where a formal 'screening' stage exists.

As Article 6(3) states, the legal requirement is for the Competent Authority to consider the effect of the plan or project either alone, or in combination with other plans or projects.

In approaching all considerations to do with the Habitats Regulation, the competent authority is required to adopt a precautionary approach

---

[111] R (on the application of Champion) v North Norfolk District Council and another [2015] 4 All ER 169

[112] In No Adastral New Town Ltd v Suffolk Coastal DC [2015] EWCA Civ 88

[113] Para 41.

towards any assessment. The European Court of Justice has adopted a strict precautionary approach to the assessment provisions of the Habitats Directive, so that *'competent national authorities are to authorise an activity on the protected site only if they have made certain that it will not adversely affect the integrity of that site' (Holohan v An Bord Pleanala).*[114] Also, in *R (on the application of Wyatt) v Fareham BC*[115] it was held that Article 6(3) embodies the precautionary principle *'and makes it possible effectively to prevent adverse effects on the integrity of protected sites as a result of the plans or projects being considered.'*

The threshold for requiring an appropriate assessment was described by the Advocate General Sharpston as '*very low*' in the case of *Sweetman v An bord Pleanala.*[116] In Waddenzee[117] it was held that the word 'likely' in the phrase 'likely to have a significant effect' meant '*such a risk exists if it cannot be excluded on the basis of objective information.*'

Appropriate Assessment

What approach needs to be taken when an appropriate authority conducts an appropriate assessment?

An appropriate assessment required in the first sentence of Article 6(3) has to identify '*all the aspects of the plan or project which can, either individually or in combination with other plans or projects, affect the conservation objectives of that site*', but it also *'cannot have lacunae and must contain complete, precise and definitive findings and conclusions capable of*

[114] *Holohan v An Bord Pleanala C-461/17*

[115] *R (on the application of Wyatt) v Fareham BC [2022] EWCA Civ 983*

[116] Sweetman v An bord Pleanala C-258/11

[117] At para 45. Landelijke Vereniging tot Behoud van de Waddenzee v Staatssecretaris van Landbouw (Coöperatieve Producentenorganisatie van de Nederlandse Kokkelvisserij UA, intervening) C-127/02.

removing all reasonable scientific doubt as to the effects of the plans or the projects proposed on the protected site concerned...'[118]

In reaching decisions in relation to an Appropriate Assessment, '*all the aspects of the plan or project which can, either individually or in combination with other plans or projects, affect those objectives must be identified in the light of the best scientific knowledge in the field.*'[119]

The generally accepted position is that competent authorities '*are entitled to place considerable weight on the opinion of Natural England, as the expert national agency with responsibility for oversight of nature conservation, and ought to do so (absent good reason why not)*'. More widely in relation to scientific evidence, '*it [scientific evidence] would not comply with the relevant standards of evidence indicated by the ECJ/CJEU for a national competent authority simply to rely for its screening opinion or "appropriate assessment" under art 6(3) on a mere assertion by an expert, unsupported by consideration of any background facts and without reasoning to explain the assertion made. If such a case arose, evidence of that* character *could fairly be described as merely subjective, and as material which failed to qualify as something which could be regarded as "the best scientific knowledge in the field".*' The scientific evidence should be '*up to date*'. (per Sales LJ in *Smyth v Secretary of State for Communities and Local Government*[120])

At what stages can mitigation be taken into account in assessing a plan or project?

---

118 Landelijke Vereniging tot Behoud van de Waddenzee v Staatssecretaris van Landbouw (Coöperatieve Producentenorganisatie van de Nederlandse Kokkelvisserij UA, intervening) C-127/02.

119 Landelijke Vereniging tot Behoud van de Waddenzee v Staatssecretaris van Landbouw (Coöperatieve Producentenorganisatie van de Nederlandse Kokkelvisserij UA, intervening) C-127/02.

120 Smyth v Secretary of State for Communities and Local Government [2015] EWCA Civ 174. (paras 82-86 and para 102)

The case-law in relation to this question addresses three distinct stages of the Habitat Directive assessment. The two stages of Article 6(3) and the position of mitigation/compensation under Article 6(4). The first stages of Article 6(3) is the determination of whether a plan or project will likely have a significant effect on the site. The second stage of Article 6(3) being a decision following an appropriate assessment.

Sales LJ in *Smyth v Secretary of State for Communities and Local Government* – in a decision taken in 2015 before the case of *Sweetman* (summarised below) – in his judgement stated *'If the competent authority can be sure from the information available at the preliminary screening stage (including information about preventive safeguarding measures) that there will be no significant harmful effects on the relevant protected site, there would be no point in proceeding to carry out an "appropriate assessment" to check the same thing. It would be disproportionate and unduly burdensome in such a case to require the national competent authority and the proposer of a project to undergo the delay, effort and expense of going through an entirely unnecessary additional stage.'*

In the 2018 case of *Sweetman v An bord Pleanala*[121] the European Court of Justice was considering the single question '*Whether measures intended to avoid or reduce the harmful effects of a plan or project on the site concerned can be taken into consideration at the screening stage, in order to determine whether it is necessary to carry out an appropriate assessment of the implications, for the site, of that plan or project?'* The Court followed the logic that since mitigatory measures were intended to avoid or reduce harmful effects to the protected site, it followed that in situations where mitigation was being applied that there had to be an underlying concern that the project would have significant harmful effects on the site. It followed from that *'Taking account of such measures at the screening stage would be liable to compromise the practical effect of the Habitats Directive in general, and the assessment stage in particular, as the latter stage would be deprived of its purpose and there would be a risk of circumvention of that*

[121] Sweetman v An bord Pleanala (C-323/17)

stage, which constitutes, however, an essential safeguard provided for by the directive.'

The High Court in *R (Langton) v Secretary of State for Communities and Local Government*[122] considered the position where badger culling licences issued by Natural England were subject to challenge. In the legal challenge to the licences it was asserted that the conditions that restricted the location of culling activity and the times of year that it could take place were mitigation and ought not to have been taken into account before an appropriate assessment. Sir Ross Cranston in giving judgement found '*In my view the licence conditions which Natural England attached to the licences in Areas 16 and 17 are not the mitigating or protective measures which featured in the 'People Over Wind' ruling. They are properly characterised as integral features of the project which Natural England needed to assess under the Habitats Regulations.*' This ruling was not tested in the Court of Appeal[123] since Natural England had amended their procedures following the ruling in *Sweetman* and successfully contended that the ground of appeal had been overtaken by events.

As to the separate question, at what stage of a planning application Habitats Directive appropriate assessments can be made? This was considered in *CG Fry and Son Ltd v Secretary of State for Levelling Up Housing and Communities and another.*[124] In that case Sir Ross Cranston determined:

> *In my view Wingfield*[125] *and Swire*[126] *are authority for the proposition that an appropriate assessment can apply at the reserved*

[122] R (Langton) v Secretary of State for Communities and Local Government [2018] EWHC 2190 (Admin)

[123] [2019] EWCA Civ 1562.

[124] CG Fry and Son Ltd v Secretary of State for Levelling Up Housing and Communities and another [2023] EWHC 1622 (Admin)

[125] R (Wingfield) v Canterbury City Council [2019] EWHC 1974 (Admin)

[126] R (Swire) v Canterbury City Council [2022] EWHC 390 (Admin)

> *matters or discharge of condition stage even if there has been a grant of outline planning permission where the subsequent approval is the implementing decision. There is support, as Lang J found in Wingfield, in the case law concerning the EIA multi-stage consenting procedure such as Barker. There, as we saw, Lord Hope recognised that a material change in circumstances could require an assessment at the reserved matters stage. It will be recalled that in Friends of the Irish Environment Ltd the CJEU stated that the meaning of "development consent" was relevant to defining the equivalent term "agree" in the Habitats Directive. All this is retained case law under the Withdrawal Act 2018 concerning the interpretation of the Habitats Directive and the Habitats Regulations 2017. That the facts in Wingfield and Swire were different is no basis for undermining the principle they established. The common law system would not survive if this were the case, since there will always be a variation, even if slight, in the facts of later cases. That does not preclude the continued application of principle.*

Detrimental activity taking place outside of protected area (SAC or SPA) is required to undergo an appropriate assessment if it is likely to have a significant effect on a separately located protected site. In *Commission v Germany*[127] there was a challenge to the German government's assessment criteria that meant that installations could be given authorisation to operate where they affected a protected site outside of the area for which the authorisation was granted. It was held that the German government had failed to properly implement Articles 6(3) and 6(4) of the Habitats Directive by not affording the protected site protection in that authorisation process.

[127] Commission v Germany Case C-98/03

The Appropriate Assessment Decision

As set out in Article 3, '*the competent national authority shall agree to the plan or project only after having ascertained that it will not adversely affect the integrity of the site concerned and, if appropriate, after having obtained the opinion of the general public.*'

In making the decision, the competent authority is able to consider mitigation measures to either eliminate or so reduce the impact of a plan or project to the extent that it no longer represents a risk of being likely to have a detrimental effect on the integrity of the protected site.

If the applicant cannot demonstrate to the competent authority that there will be no effect on the integrity of the site, the competent authority must reject the application unless the applicant can demonstrate that there are 'imperative reasons of overriding public interest.' ('IROPI')

Article 6(4)/Regulation 64 – IROPI derogation

The first consideration if IROPI is being advanced is whether there are alternative solutions.[128] An example of this was the Secretary of State's refusal in 2004 to grant the expansion of the port facilities in Southampton proposed in Dibden Bay on the basis that there had been no assessment of alternative facilities at other ports on the south and east coasts. The considerations of the Secretary of State would include the answer to the question whether the alternatives were both feasible while delivering less harm. In assessing the alternatives available, these are to be measured against the objectives of the plan or project and should include consideration of all reasonable objectives capable of meeting the relevant objective.[129]

---

[128] Regulation 64(1).

[129] R (on the application of Friends of the Earth) v Welsh Ministers [2015] EWHC 776 (Admin)

The second consideration, if IROPI is being advanced, is to determine whether the site contains a priority natural habitat or priority species. The Habitats Regulations demonstrate that very narrow considerations apply in those circumstances.

Regulation 64 (2) Where the site concerned hosts a priority natural habitat type or a priority species, the reasons referred to in paragraph (1) must be either—

(a) reasons relating to human health, public safety or beneficial consequences of primary importance to the environment; or

(b) any other reasons which the competent authority, having due regard to the opinion of the appropriate authority, considers to be imperative reasons of overriding public interest.

In the IROPI decision-making process, the applicant would need to demonstrate that there was an imperative underlying the application. It would clearly need to show that the plan or project is necessary. In that regard it may consider social and economic benefits. The imperative must be overriding in that the interests of the project outweigh the harm to the site. Finally it must be in the public interest that the project or plan is implemented, rather than solely a private interest.

Article 6(4) and Compensation

Notwithstanding the provisions of Article 3 of the Habitats Directive, a plan or project may be approved if, in spite of a negative assessment of the implications for the site and in the absence if alternative solutions, a plan or project must nevertheless be carried out for imperative reasons of overriding public interest, including those of a social or economic nature, the Member State shall take all compensatory measures necessary to ensure that the overall coherence of Natura 2000 is protected.[130]

These 'IROPI" provisions are significant as they represent a different and higher test, not least because the provisions acknowledge that a site of national importance is being harmed by the plan or project in question.

Mitigation and Compensation

Dealing with Articles 6(3) and 6(4) Habitat Directive will often involve a discussion around whether what is being proposed to ameliorate the harm caused by a plan or project amounts to mitigation or compensation.

T C Briels and Others v Minister van Infrastructuur en Milieu[131] considered whether the creation of replacement (and additional) protected 'molina meadows' habitat, part of which was proposed to be destroyed by a motorway project, would constitute mitigation under Article 6(3) or compensation under Article 6(4) of the Habitats Regulations.

At para 31 of the judgement the following was stated *'It is clear that these measures are not aimed either at avoiding or reducing the significant adverse effects for that habitat type caused by the A2 motorway project; rather, they tend to compensate after the fact for those effects. They do not guarantee that the project will not adversely affect the integrity of the site within the meaning of Article 6(3) of the Habitats Directive.'*

The distinction as between mitigation and compensation is significant. It was stated in Briels:

> *...protective measures provided for in a project which are aimed at compensating for the negative effects of the project on a Natura 2000*

---

[130] The same obligation remains on the UK authorities in relation to 'National Site Network' sites.

[131] T C Briels and Others v Minister van Infrastructuur en Milieu *C-521/12*

> *site cannot be taken into account in the assessment of the implications of the project provided for in article 6(3).*

In *Smyth v Secretary of State for Communities and Local Government*[132] Sales LJ set out the difference as between mitigation measures – designed to mitigate or eliminate possible adverse effects or compensation measures where some form of environmental enhancement at another location is used to replace harm to a site. In relation to mitigatory measure he stated (at para 65):

> *As to (a) [whether any measures designed to mitigate or eliminate possible adverse effects on a protected site from a plan or project may be taken into account within art 6(3) of the Habitats Directive, as distinct from being relevant under art 6(4)], in my judgment it is clear that preventive safeguarding measures which have the effect of eliminating completely or mitigating to some degree possible harmful effects of a plan or project on a protected site (in the sense that they prevent such effects from arising at all or to some degree) may be taken into account under art 6(3), and a competent authority is not confined to bringing them into account under art 6(4).*

The learned judge continued (at para 68):

> *On the other hand, where measures are proposed which would not prevent harm from occurring, but which would (once harm to a protected site has occurred) provide some form of off-setting compensation so that the harm to the site is compensated by new environmental enhancing measures elsewhere, then it cannot be said that those off-setting measures prevent harm from occurring so as to meet the preventive and precautionary objectives of art 6(3). In the case of off-setting measures, the competent authority is asked to allow harm to a protected site to occur, on the basis that this harm will be counter-balanced and offset by other measures to enhance the*

---

132 Smyth v Secretary of State for Communities and Local Government [2015] EWCA Civ 174. (paras 64-77)

environment elsewhere or in other ways. In order to allow the harm to a protected site which art 6(3) is supposed to ensure does not occur, a competent authority will have to be satisfied that such harm can be justified under art 6(4), taking account of the off-setting compensation measures at the stage of analysis under art 6(4). Such measures would not be capable of bearing on the application of the tests under art 6(3), and so could not be relevant at the art 6(3) stage.

Sales LJ continued to say that in Smyth (para 77):

The Inspector was lawfully entitled to take into account the proposed preventive safeguarding measures in respect of the SPA and SAC under the first limb of art 6(3), for the purposes of giving a screening opinion to the effect that no "appropriate assessment" would be required under the second limb of art 6(3), in the course of his consideration whether to grant planning permission.

The case of *Smyth* (2015) pre-dated *Grace v An bord Pleanala*[133] (2019). It is notable that the judgement in *Grace* was given on 25th July 2018, and is therefore a binding authority.

The judgement included:

50. In that regard, the Court has previously ruled that the measures provided for in a project which are aimed at compensating for the negative effects of the project cannot be taken into account in the assessment of the implications of the project provided for in Article 6(3) of the Habitats Directive (judgments of 15 May 2014, Briels and Others, C-521/12, EU:C:2014:330, paragraph 29, and of 21 July 2016, Orleans and Others, C-387/15 and C-388/15, EU:C:2016:583, paragraph 48).

51 It is only when it is sufficiently certain that a measure will make an effective contribution to avoiding harm, guaranteeing beyond

[133] Grace v An bord Pleanala (C-164/17)

all reasonable doubt that the project will not adversely affect the integrity of the area, that such a measure may be taken into consideration when the appropriate assessment is carried out (see, to that effect, judgment of 26 April 2017, Commission v Germany, C-142/16, EU:C:2017:301, paragraph 38).

52 As a general rule, any positive effects of the future creation of a new habitat, which is aimed at compensating for the loss of area and quality of that habitat type in a protected area, are highly difficult to forecast with any degree of certainty or will be visible only in the future (see, to that effect, judgment of 21 July 2016, Orleans and Others, C-387/15 and C-388/15, EU:C:2016:583, paragraphs 52 and 56 and the case-law cited).

53 It is not the fact that the habitat concerned in the main proceedings is in constant flux and that that area requires 'dynamic' management that is the cause of uncertainty. In fact, such uncertainty is the result of the identification of adverse effects, certain or potential, on the integrity of the area concerned as a habitat and foraging area and, therefore, on one of the constitutive characteristics of that area, and of the inclusion in the assessment of the implications of future benefits to be derived from the adoption of measures which, at the time that assessment is made, are only potential, as the measures have not yet been implemented. Accordingly, and subject to verifications to be carried out by the referring court, it was not possible for those benefits to be foreseen with the requisite degree of certainty when the authorities approved the contested development.

And at para 57:

57 It follows that the answer to the question referred is that Article 6 of the Habitats

> *Directive must be interpreted as meaning that, where it is intended to carry out a project on a site designated for the protection and conservation of certain species, of which the area suitable for providing for the needs of a protected species fluctuates over time, and the temporary or permanent effect of that project will be that some parts of the site will no longer be able to provide a suitable habitat for the species in question, the fact that the project includes measures to ensure that, after an appropriate assessment of the implications of the project has been carried out and throughout the lifetime of the project, the part of the site that is in fact likely to provide a suitable habitat will not be reduced and indeed may be enhanced may not be taken into account for the purpose of the assessment that must be carried out in accordance with Article 6(3) of the directive to ensure that the project in question will not adversely affect the integrity of the site concerned; that fact falls to be considered, if need be, under Article 6(4) of the directive.*

The judgement gives a clear steer that even in circumstances where it is certain that measures included within the project put it beyond a reasonable doubt that the project will not adversely affect the integrity of the area, that such measures need to be factored into the appropriate assessment stage. The judgement suggests that such projects cannot be eliminated in the first stage test of the Article 6(3) tests.

CHAPTER SIX

HABITAT AND BIODIVERSITY TRENDS

The United Nations Environment Programme states the following in relation to biodiversity:

> *Biological diversity is the variety of life on Earth and the natural patterns it forms. The biodiversity seen today is the result of 4.5 billion years of evolution and, increasingly, of human influence as well. It forms the web of life, of which humans are integral and upon which people and the planet so fully depend.*
>
> ***Biodiversity breakdown***
>
> *Species are now disappearing hundreds, or even thousands, of times faster than the natural background rate of extinction. The scientific community has repeatedly sounded the alarm on the triple planetary crisis of climate change, nature and biodiversity loss, and pollution and waste.*

Within the UK the statutory bodies, the Joint Nature Conservation Committee, Natural England, Natural Resources Wales, NatureScot and the Northern Ireland Environment Agency, jointly published 'Nature Positive 2030' in 2021 in which they stated:

> *Globally, over 1 million species are threatened with extinction and the populations of many animals have declined by at least two-thirds since 1970. Here in the UK, 40% of species are in decline, more than 40 million birds have been lost from our skies over the past 50 years, and a quarter of mammals are threatened with extinction including many once common species, such as the hedgehog. These ongoing declines, on top of earlier losses since the industrial revolution has led to the UK*

> *becoming one of the most nature-depleted nations on Earth. We still have many important habitats and species, and beautiful patches of nature to enjoy, but these are a shadow of what we would have if we recovered nature.*

Evidence from the scientific body as to the depletion of biodiversity and habitats suggests that current legislation has, at best, slowed the pace of environmental harm. It has not been adequate to stop or reverse such harm.

The historic, and by-and-large current, legislative and regulatory framework is defensive in nature. It is structured around trying to control activity that is harmful to the environment by seeking to reduce and mitigate any harm caused by development or permitted activity. Such an approach has undoubtably acted to slow any environmental harm caused, but it has not prevented it.

In recognition of this failure, the legislative narrative has changed in recent times with a view to reversing the historic trend.

Biodiversity Net Gain

The Environment Act 2021 introduced biodiversity net gain requirements into the planning regime with Section 98 simply stating *'Schedule 14 makes provision for biodiversity gain to be a condition of planning permission in England.'* Similar provision is made by Section 99 for biodiversity gain in nationally significant infrastructure projects.

Schedule 14 amends the Town and Country Planning Act 1990 by adding a Section 90A that brings into effect a new Schedule 7A of the Town and Country Planning Act 1990. That schedule makes provision for the conditioning of biodiversity net gain within the planning process.

Schedule 7A, paragraph 2 sets out the following provisions:

(1) *The biodiversity gain objective is met in relation to development for which planning permission is granted if the biodiversity value attributable to the development exceeds the pre-development biodiversity value of the onsite habitat by at least the relevant percentage.*

(2) *The biodiversity value attributable to the development is the total of—*

(a) *the post-development biodiversity value of the onsite habitat,*

(b) *the biodiversity value, in relation to the development, of any registered offsite biodiversity gain allocated to the development, and*

(c) *the biodiversity value of any biodiversity credits purchased for the development.*

(3) *The relevant percentage is 10%.*

Paragraph 6 provides protection against efforts to frustrate the process:

If—

(a) *a person carries on activities on land on or after 30 January 2020 otherwise than in accordance with—*

(i) *planning permission, or*

(ii) *any other permission of a kind specified by the Secretary of State by regulations, and*

(b) *as a result of the activities the biodiversity value of the onsite habitat referred to in paragraph 5(1) is lower on the relevant date than it would otherwise have been, the pre-development biodiversity value of the onsite habitat is to be taken to be its*

> *biodiversity value immediately before the carrying on of the activities.*

Section 100 allows the Secretary of State to set up a 'register of biodiversity net gain sites:'

> *(2) A biodiversity gain site is land where—*
>
> > *(a) a person is required under a conservation covenant or planning obligation to carry out works for the purpose of habitat enhancement,*
> >
> > *(b) that or another person is required to maintain the enhancement for at least 30 years after the completion of those works, and*
> >
> > *(c) for the purposes of Schedule 7A to the Town and Country Planning Act 1990 the enhancement is made available to be allocated (conditionally or unconditionally, and whether for consideration or otherwise) in accordance with the terms of the covenant or obligation to one or more developments for which planning permission is granted.*

Where land cannot be directly identified, the Secretary of State, pursuant to Section 101, can set up a system of biodiversity credits.

Biodiversity net gain provisions have already been included within marine plans, as 'marine net gain'.

Rural Payments

Another central regulatory instrument that is being used by the Government in relation to habitat protection is altering the structure of the Rural Payments Scheme with the introduction of the Sustainable Farming Initiative. The Government has also announced the Local

Nature Recovery Scheme and the Landscape Recovery Scheme. If successfully implemented, such schemes that affect a significant part of the UK landscape, are capable of significantly influencing habitat and wildlife protection and recovery.

MORE BOOKS BY LAW BRIEF PUBLISHING

'A Practical Guide to Bad Character Evidence for Criminal Practitioners by Aparna Rao
'A Practical Guide to Extradition Law post-Brexit' by Myles Grandison et al
'A Practical Guide to Hoarding and Mental Health for Housing Lawyers' by Rachel Coyle
'A Practical Guide to Psychiatric Claims in Personal Injury – 2nd Edition' by Liam Ryan
'Stephens on Contractual Indemnities' by Richard Stephens
'A Practical Guide to the EU Succession Regulation' by Richard Frimston
'A Practical Guide to Solicitor and Client Costs – 2nd Edition' by Robin Dunne
'Constructive Dismissal – Practice Pointers and Principles' by Benjimin Burgher
'A Practical Guide to Religion and Belief Discrimination Claims in the Workplace' by Kashif Ali
'A Practical Guide to the Law of Medical Treatment Decisions' by Ben Troke
'Fundamental Dishonesty and QOCS in Personal Injury Proceedings: Law and Practice' by Jake Rowley
'A Practical Guide to the Law in Relation to School Exclusions' by Charlotte Hadfield & Alice de Coverley
'A Practical Guide to Divorce for the Silver Separators' by Karin Walker
'The Right to be Forgotten – The Law and Practical Issues' by Melissa Stock
'A Practical Guide to Planning Law and Rights of Way in National Parks, the Broads and AONBs' by James Maurici QC, James Neill et al
'A Practical Guide to Election Law' by Tom Tabori
'A Practical Guide to the Law in Relation to Surrogacy' by Andrew Powell
'A Practical Guide to Claims Arising from Fatal Accidents – 2nd Edition' by James Patience
'A Practical Guide to the Ownership of Employee Inventions – From Entitlement to Compensation' by James Tumbridge & Ashley Roughton
'A Practical Guide to Asbestos Claims' by Jonathan Owen & Gareth McAloon
'A Practical Guide to Stamp Duty Land Tax in England and Northern Ireland' by Suzanne O'Hara
'A Practical Guide to the Law of Farming Partnerships' by Philip Whitcomb
'Covid-19, Homeworking and the Law – The Essential Guide to Employment and GDPR Issues' by Forbes Solicitors
'Covid-19 and Criminal Law – The Essential Guide' by Ramya Nagesh

'Covid-19 and Family Law in England and Wales – The Essential Guide' by Safda Mahmood
'A Practical Guide to the Law of Unlawful Eviction and Harassment – 2nd Edition' by Stephanie Lovegrove
'Covid-19, Brexit and the Law of Commercial Leases – The Essential Guide' by Mark Shelton
'A Practical Guide to Costs in Personal Injury Claims – 2nd Edition' by Matthew Hoe
'A Practical Guide to the General Data Protection Regulation (GDPR) – 2nd Edition' by Keith Markham
'Ellis on Credit Hire – Sixth Edition' by Aidan Ellis & Tim Kevan
'A Practical Guide to Working with Litigants in Person and McKenzie Friends in Family Cases' by Stuart Barlow
'Protecting Unregistered Brands: A Practical Guide to the Law of Passing Off' by Lorna Brazell
'A Practical Guide to Secondary Liability and Joint Enterprise Post-Jogee' by Joanne Cecil & James Mehigan
'A Practical Guide to the Pre-Action RTA Claims Protocol for Personal Injury Lawyers' by Antonia Ford
'A Practical Guide to Neighbour Disputes and the Law' by Alexander Walsh
'A Practical Guide to Forfeiture of Leases' by Mark Shelton
'A Practical Guide to Coercive Control for Legal Practitioners and Victims' by Rachel Horman
'A Practical Guide to Rights Over Airspace and Subsoil' by Daniel Gatty
'Tackling Disclosure in the Criminal Courts – A Practitioner's Guide' by Narita Bahra QC & Don Ramble
'A Practical Guide to the Law of Driverless Cars – Second Edition' by Alex Glassbrook, Emma Northey & Scarlett Milligan
'A Practical Guide to TOLATA Claims' by Greg Williams
'A Practical Guide to Elderly Law – 2nd Edition' by Justin Patten
'A Practical Guide to Responding to Housing Disrepair and Unfitness Claims' by Iain Wightwick
'A Practical Guide to the Construction and Rectification of Wills and Trust Instruments' by Edward Hewitt
'A Practical Guide to the Law of Bullying and Harassment in the Workplace' by Philip Hyland

'How to Be a Freelance Solicitor: A Practical Guide to the SRA-Regulated Freelance Solicitor Model' by Paul Bennett
'A Practical Guide to Prison Injury Claims' by Malcolm Johnson
'A Practical Guide to the Small Claims Track - 2nd Edition' by Dominic Bright
'A Practical Guide to Advising Clients at the Police Station' by Colin Stephen McKeown-Beaumont
'A Practical Guide to Antisocial Behaviour Injunctions' by Iain Wightwick
'Practical Mediation: A Guide for Mediators, Advocates, Advisers, Lawyers, and Students in Civil, Commercial, Business, Property, Workplace, and Employment Cases' by Jonathan Dingle with John Sephton
'The Mini-Pupillage Workbook' by David Boyle
'A Practical Guide to Crofting Law' by Brian Inkster
'A Practical Guide to Spousal Maintenance' by Liz Cowell
'A Practical Guide to the Law of Domain Names and Cybersquatting' by Andrew Clemson
'A Practical Guide to the Law of Gender Pay Gap Reporting' by Harini Iyengar
'NHS Whistleblowing and the Law' by Joseph England
'Employment Law and the Gig Economy' by Nigel Mackay & Annie Powell
'A Practical Guide to Noise Induced Hearing Loss (NIHL) Claims' by Andrew Mckie, Ian Skeate, Gareth McAloon
'An Introduction to Beauty Negligence Claims – A Practical Guide for the Personal Injury Practitioner' by Greg Almond
'Intercompany Agreements for Transfer Pricing Compliance' by Paul Sutton
'Zen and the Art of Mediation' by Martin Plowman
'A Practical Guide to the SRA Principles, Individual and Law Firm Codes of Conduct 2019 – What Every Law Firm Needs to Know' by Paul Bennett
'A Practical Guide to Adoption for Family Lawyers' by Graham Pegg
'A Practical Guide to Industrial Disease Claims' by Andrew Mckie & Ian Skeate
'A Practical Guide to Redundancy' by Philip Hyland
'A Practical Guide to Vicarious Liability' by Mariel Irvine
'A Practical Guide to Applications for Landlord's Consent and Variation of Leases' by Mark Shelton
'A Practical Guide to Relief from Sanctions Post-Mitchell and Denton' by Peter Causton

'A Practical Guide to Equity Release for Advisors' by Paul Sams
'A Practical Guide to Financial Services Claims' by Chris Hegarty
'The Law of Houses in Multiple Occupation: A Practical Guide to HMO Proceedings' by Julian Hunt
'Occupiers, Highways and Defective Premises Claims: A Practical Guide Post-Jackson – 2nd Edition' by Andrew Mckie
'A Practical Guide to Financial Ombudsman Service Claims' by Adam Temple & Robert Scrivenor
'A Practical Guide to Advising Schools on Employment Law' by Jonathan Holden
'A Practical Guide to Running Housing Disrepair and Cavity Wall Claims: 2nd Edition' by Andrew Mckie & Ian Skeate
'A Practical Guide to Holiday Sickness Claims – 2nd Edition' by Andrew Mckie & Ian Skeate
'Arguments and Tactics for Personal Injury and Clinical Negligence Claims' by Dorian Williams
'A Practical Guide to Drone Law' by Rufus Ballaster, Andrew Firman, Eleanor Clot
'A Practical Guide to Compliance for Personal Injury Firms Working With Claims Management Companies' by Paul Bennett
'RTA Allegations of Fraud in a Post-Jackson Era: The Handbook – 2nd Edition' by Andrew Mckie
'RTA Personal Injury Claims: A Practical Guide Post-Jackson' by Andrew Mckie
'On Experts: CPR35 for Lawyers and Experts' by David Boyle
'An Introduction to Personal Injury Law' by David Boyle

These books and more are available to order online direct from the publisher at www.lawbriefpublishing.com, where you can also read free sample chapters. For any queries, contact us on 0844 587 2383 or mail@lawbriefpublishing.com.

Our books are also usually in stock at www.amazon.co.uk with free next day delivery for Prime members, and at good legal bookshops such as Wildy & Sons.

We are regularly launching new books in our series of practical day-to-day practitioners' guides. Visit our website and join our free newsletter to be kept informed and to receive special offers, free chapters, etc.

You can also follow us on Twitter at www.twitter.com/lawbriefpub.

www.ingramcontent.com/pod-product-compliance
Ingram Content Group UK Ltd.
Pitfield, Milton Keynes, MK11 3LW, UK
UKHW020148290926
15471UKWH00004B/749

9 781914 608865